DIRECTORY
of
U.S. ARMY
FORTS, CAMPS,
& AIRFIELDS
(1789 to 1945)

By Tom Kneitel

CRB Research Books, Inc.

P.O. Box 56, Commack, New York 11725

Respectfully dedicated, with appreciation, to:
All of the officers and enlisted personnel who
proudly served our country in the United States Army.

Cover and book design by Robin Smith.

Printed in the United States of America.

ISBN: 0-939780-16-X

Introduction

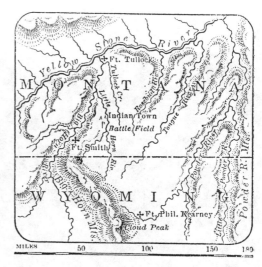

This is an unofficial listing compiled from a variety of official and unofficial sources. Its primary goal is to provide a guide, with locations, to named United States Army forts, camps, airfields, cantonments, redoubts, and batteries that were established between the time of the United States Army's organization (September 29, 1789) and the end of World War II, in 1945.

No deliberate attempt has been made to include the equivalent facilities operated by other military services, nor unnamed United States Army facilities, nor short-term bivouac or encampment areas or battlefield posts.

The Posts Listed Herein

Many of the forts and structures named were erected by the early settlers for their own protection, and all obvious vestiges of them vanished long ago. The exact locations of many are not known at the present time, but references are made to them in old documents, histories, and correspondence. At times, such references conflict with one another, or are vague, or offer several spelling variations for what is apparently the same facility. Moreover, when locations are given for early forts and camps, they are not always in terms immediately recognizable to the modern observer.

This is because many old locations make reference to communities, rivers, geographic features, or landmarks, streets, or structures that no longer exist, or may exist today under names that are either spelled differently, or which have been changed completely. Some of the sites given, in fact, may be local nicknames used only within a very limited geographic area, and in the long-ago past.

As such, it is not always easy to pick an early facility at random, and then quickly trace down its exact, or even general, location on a modern map or atlas. The serious searcher can employ old maps; the services of historical societies, libraries, and newspaper files, in order to pick up the trail. Conversations with local amateur historians are often invaluable.

What's There?

The forts and camps listed herein fall into different categories. As mentioned, many have faded into history without leaving any obvious traces. A trace need not be obvious in order to exist, as proven by the fact that bits and pieces of the Battle of The Little Big Horn (1876) were unearthed from the field of battle more than a hundred years later.

Camp Upton, 1917: learning how to dig trenches.

Keep in mind that sites in areas such as the southwestern states will have had a better chance of survival than those in areas like the northeast. Notwithstanding the crush of encroaching population in some areas of the nation, severe winters filled with snow and ice storms certainly are not as conducive to preserving old structures as is the arid climate of the southwest.

Although one might seek out and study old army sites anywhere in the nation, forgive me for leaning heavily on a few examples within reasonably close range of my own home base in New York State. These are the most familar to me, but they are undoubtedly typical of what you can find within a few hours drive of your own location.

There are historic sites that, although long abandoned and in ruin, still exist to one extent or another. It may be that they aren't easily accessible, or are on private or federal land that is posted against trespassing. In the author's own area, the former Fort Michie, has been abandoned since the 1920's. With the exception of the fact that its giant guns (including a 16-inch cannon that could lob a one ton shell almost 25 miles) have been removed, the facility is remarkably well preserved. It's the only thing on tiny Great Gull Island, seven miles east of Orient Point, the northeastern tip of Long Island. Not a very easy place to visit since the wooden dock is long gone, and the island is ringed with a "beach" consisting of more than twenty feet worth of large rocks that discourge impromptu boat arrivals.

Fort Tyler was built during the Spanish American War on a thin spit of beach at the northern tip of Gardiner's Island, which lies between the two forks at the eastern end of Long Island. Fort Tyler was abandoned by the military in 1924, but during World War II the U.S. Navy found it to be a handy target for its artillery crews to practice on. So, although it's still there, it has been heavily damaged. And, Gardiner's Island (rumored to be one of the places pirate Captain Kidd buried some of his treasure) is still privately owned and posted against trespassers.

4

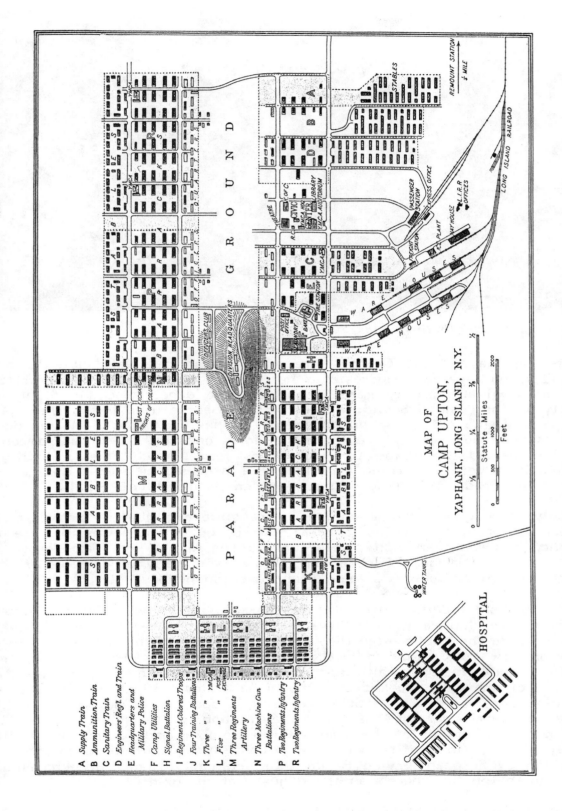

A Supply Train
B Ammunition Train
C Sanitary Train
D Engineers Regt. and Train
E Headquarters and
   Military Police
F Camp Utilities
H Signal Battalion
I Regiment Colored Troops
J Four Training Battalions
K Three   "   "
L Five   "   "
M Three Regiments
   Artillery
N Three Machine Gun
   Battalions
P Two Regiments Infantry
R Two Regiments Infantry

MAP OF
CAMP UPTON,
YAPHANK, LONG ISLAND, N.Y.

Statute Miles

Feet

Camp Upton, Yaphank, NY, in WWI. Now it's Brookhaven National Labs.

5

On the Camp Upton rifle range, 1917.

Forts Salonga and St. George were once located relatively close to my home base. Today, no apparent vestiges of either remain, although the name Fort Salonga remains on town and county maps to indicate the general location of an upscale community on Long Island Sound. Where Fort St. George used to be, there is now a county park. Using old maps and documents, it has been possible to pin down and visit the specific locations where the actual forts once stood. But if someone went looking for the old site of the Army Air Corps' former Mitchel Field, all they would find would be a college campus, a park, and a large sports arena. But at least the site offers the Cradle of Aviation Museum, which recalls Mitchel Field.

Luckily, throughout the nation, there are quite a number of historic forts that have been restored, and are not only maintained, but are museums that are open to the public. You can then visit places such as The Alamo, Fort Ticonderoga, Castle San Marcos (Fort Marion), Fort William Henry, and many other sites of the most vivid chapters in our country's colorful and exciting history.

There are old facilities that are, of course, still in use by the United States Army, or others. Naturally, they have been modernized over the years. Still, those that are open to the public often display touches from the distant past. Some of the facilities on New York's Governor's Island, Fort Hamilton, Fort Schuyler, and Fort Totten are quite historic, although the installations are still in use. At the Department of Energy's Brookhaven National Laboratory, which is located at the old Camp Upton site, modern physicists are using a spectacular device called RHIC to generate sub-atomic particles to study the creation of the universe. You can still see the decaying remains of the army's Camp Upton-- made famous in the 1918 hit Broadway show, "Yip Yip Yaphank," a "musical mess cooked up for the boys of Camp Upton by Sergeant Irving Berlin." Unfortunately, today Brookhaven Labs is off limits to the public; there's an armed guard at the gate!

A lot of the United States Army's Air Fields (AAF's), which were so numerous

6

Abandoned building, 1991. At former Suffolk County AAF.

These deserted buildings face a runway at the old Suffolk County AAF.

The old Suffolk County AAF is a modern-day ghost town. This photo was taken by the author in October of '91.

throught World War II, were transferred from the Army Air Corps in 1947, and into the newly created United States Air Force. As such, they continue to this day to serve our national defense needs. Other AAF's were either abandoned, or became civilian airports, both large and small. This opens the way for interesting exploration, for these facilities are mostly still able to be located and explored. Some are quite interesting.

In my own area, during World War II, the Army Air Corps built the Suffolk County AAF in Westhampton Beach. While far from being the most formidable military facility in the world, it was a large facility with two 5,000 ft. runways and a 9,000 ft. runway, all of concrete and 150 ft. wide. A tall concrete control tower rose from the field, as well as light towers and numerous barracks, hangars, and other structures. There was a church, a fire house, a theatre, an officers' club, BOQ's, administrative buildings, and much more, including sidewalks and a grid of roads.

For a while, after the war, the U.S. Air Force operated the facility. At some point, perhaps in the mid-to-late 1950's, the Air Force pulled out and the field became the property of the county. Today, the county operates it as a general aviation field, but it is greatly underutilized. A closed-off (to the public) part of the field is in use by the New York Air Guard's 106th Aerospace Rescue and Recovery Group. As for the rest of the facility, although in a state of graceful decay, it appears virtually the same as it probably did when it was built in World War II!

A few of the old wooden buildings have been torn down, and some have been rented out to area businesses. But, for the most part, you can drive through the deserted streets and look at the old wooden and cinder block buildings just as they

A long unused wooden lookout tower still stands near the old Suffolk County AAF. The trucks around its base belong to an industrial company leasing the property for its operations.

When the Army Air Corps turned over the Suffolk County AAF to the USAF, it became the Suffolk County AFB. That facility has been gone for decades, but this rusting USAF warning sign still adorns the side of one of the buildings near the runways.

9

This looks like it might have been the bus terminal at what once was the Suffolk County AAF. Grass now grows in the pavement cracks.

were in the 1940's and 1950's-- except considerably more shabby in their state of abandonment. There are many other facilities just like this one, perhaps several only an hour or two from your own location, if you take the trouble to look. It's an unforgettable trip through time. At what used to be the Suffolk County AAF, everybody is now welcome to drive right through the main gate. A guard no longer stands in the main gate house.

Remember though, that all such facilities are a part of history. I like to visit them with no more than a camera, carrying away with me the memories of what I saw and a batch of photographic images. Some old facilities I have visited show signs of vandalism and/or souvenir hunters. It's cruel to wantonly deface or destroy these proud old warriors, thus taking away their dignity and the possibilities for others to fully enjoy exploring them in the future.

Some people like to use metal detectors, or small gardening tools to locate small objects hidden beneath the ground surface of these facilities. I don't have any qualms about that, so long as those in charge of the facility (or its owners, if on private property) have been asked for permission and say it's OK. And, of course, that any parts of the soil that are dug up, are neatly replaced when the searching is finished. There are old bottles, buttons, tools, parts, and all sorts of other small items of interest that have been found by diligent looking. But again, don't dig, or even trespass, without proper permission.

The Facilities

Army Air Fields were usually given the names of the communities in which they were located, although larger facilities were named after notable flyers, or military personnel who died in action or air crashes. Forts, camps, and other installations

10

were usually named after locations, notable military or political personalities, or given names relating to their duties or to heroic attributes. Certain popular names have been recycled and used many times over and over again at different installations during several time periods. Installations may undergo a complete name change, and there are Camps that were upgrated to the status of Forts.

Keeping track of all of this means that there are inevitable omissions, errors, and duplications. The author enthusiastically seeks additional input regarding such matters, and is always pleased to receive clarifying information, as well as suggestions, for use in the preparation of any future revised editions. The author may be contacted in care of the publisher of this book.

The author would here like to specifically acknowledge the pioneering research in this field done many decades ago by historian Francis B. Heitman. In 1903, Heitman's exhaustive research on 18th and 19th Century United States Army forts and camps was the first and only work of its kind. Heitman's great wealth of information has now at last been somewhat reorganized, corrected when required, and incorporated into this new work so that researchers, military historians, archaeologists, students, tourists, shutterbugs, buried artifact hunters, trivia buffs, the incurably curious, and other interested parties can still make use of the fascinating and valuable data that took Heitman so many years to compile.

Bibliography

Alsberg, Henry G.; The American Guide, Hastings House, New York, 1949.
Commerce, U.S. Dept. of; Commercial and Government Radio Stations of The United States, U.S. Government Printing Office, 1924, 1928, 1930, 1931 editions.
Commerce, U.S. Dept. of; Sectional Aeronautical Charts, all areas of U.S., 1943.
Consolidated Telegraph Company; Consolidated Radio Call Book, New York, 1919.
Cragg, Sgt. Dan (U.S. Army, Ret.); Guide to Military Installations, 2nd Edition, Stackpole Books, Harrisburg, PA, 1988.
DeWan, George; Ruins of War, Newsday Magazine, New York, February 14, 1988.
Heitman, Francis B.; Historical Register & Dictionary of the United States Army, 1789-1903, Government Printing Office, 1903.
International Telecommunications Union; Berne List of Frequencies, Berne Switzerland, 1933 to 1947 editions.
Stewart, George R.; American Place Names, Oxford University Press, New York, 1970.
War Department; Joint Army/Navy Publication #JANP-114, Call Letters of Land Stations of The Armed Forces, 1944.

Also, numerous newspapers and periodicals from 1900 to 1945, as well as personal correspondence.

*Irving Berlin's musical "Yip Yip Yaphank"
was written during and about his WWI
experiences at Camp Upton, on Long Island.*

Camp Wickoff (or Wyckoff), Long Island, in 1898.

Pres. James Madison

Infantryman's route march.

★★★

Status of American Forts at the Beginning of The War of 1812.
Excerpted from the book, "A Popular History of The United States of America,"
by John Clark Ridpath, A.M., LL.D. (Phillips & Hunt, N.Y., 1884)

It became apparent that the war was destined to be a conflict on the seacoast and the ocean. The United States would act for the most part on the defensive, and Great Britain would rely chiefly upon her navy. The condition of both nations was such as to provoke this sort of warfare. On the one side was the British armament superior to any other in the world, and on the other an exposed seacoast, a few fortresses, and a navy of almost insignificant proportions.

From the beginning, the policy of the American government had been distinctly declared against a standing army and a regular fleet. It was held that a citizen soldiery and an extemporized flotilla would be sufficient for every emergency. A large military establishment, said the defenders of the American system, is enormously expensive and a constant nuisance to civil liberty. After the Revolution, especially during the administration of Jefferson, the military spirit was discouraged and the defenses of the country fell into decay. In 1808 the whole coast of Maine was defended only by Fort Sumner, at Portland. New Hampshire had but one fortress, a half-ruined blockhouse at at Portsmouth. On the coast of Massachusetts four fortifications-- one at Cape Ann, one at Salem, one at Marblehead, and Fort Independence in Boston Harbor-- furnished the only security against attack. In the neighborhood of Newport, Rhode Island, there were six works, some of importance, others insignificant. New London, Connecticut, was defended by Fort Trumbull, a block-house of considerable strength but in bad repair. On Governor's Island, in the harbor at New York, stood Fort Jay, which, together with the Battery at the south end of Manhattan and some slight fortifications on Ellis's and Bedloe's Islands, furnished a tolerable protection. The whole coast of New Jersey lay open to invasion. On Mud Island in the Delaware, a short distance below Philadelphia, stood the formidible Fort Mifflin, an old British fort of the Revolution. Not less in strength and importance was Fort McHenry on the Patapsco, commanding the approach to Baltimore. Annapolis was defended by Fort Severn, then only a group of breast-works. Norfolk, Virginia, relied for protection on a fort of the same name and another work, called Fort Nelson, on the opposite side of the Elizabeth River. In the harbor at Charleston stood Fort Johnson on James's Island, Fort Pinckney in front of the city, and Fort Moultrie of Revolutionary fame. Upon these scattered fortifications and the terror inspired by Fulton's torpedoes the Americans must depend for the defense of a coastline reaching from the Passamaquoddy to the St. Mary's.

★★★

WWI rookies getting in shape at Fort Hancock.

A Signal Corps training exercise during WWI.

Some Military, Political, & Other Personalities Whose Names Have Been Used For U.S. Army Forts, Camps, & Air Fields

Custer

McClellan

Andrews, Lt. Frank M., killed in a 1943 air crash.

Barksdale, Lt. Eugene H., died in a 1926 air crash.

Beale, Gen. Edward F., who suggested that camels be used for army transportation.

Beauregard, Gen. Pierre, Confederate Army, 1818-1893, ordered the bombing of Ft. Sumter that began the Civil War.

Benning, Maj. Gen. Henry L., Confederate Army.

Bliss, William W.S.

Bolling, Col. Raynal C., killed in WWI.

Boone, Daniel, 1734-1820, frontiersman.

Bragg, Gen. Braxton, Confederate Army.

Bridger, James, trapper and mountain man.

Brooks, Cadet Sidney, Jr., killed in a 1942 air crash.

Butler, Benjamin F., 1818-1893, army officer and Congressman.

Campbell, Gen. William B., a hero of the Mexican War.

Carson, Kit, frontier scout.

Carswell, Maj. Horace S., WWII Medal of Honor recipient.

Castle, Brig. Gen Frederick W., killed leading an air raid over Germany during WWII.

Chanute, Octave, a pioneer aviation engineer.

Clark, George R., 1752-1818, commissioned by Patrick Henry to conquer Illinois.

Crockett, Davey, 1786-1836, frontiersman, politician, and a hero of The Alamo.

Custer, Gen. George A., 1839-1876, killed at the Little Big Horn.

Dade, Maj. F. L., killed in Seminole Wars, 1835.

Davis-Monthan: Lt. Samuel H. Davis, killed in 1921 air crash; Lt. Oscar Monthan, killed in a 1927 air crash.

Devens, Maj. Gen. Charles, USA, Civil War, also served as Attorney General of the United States.

Dix, Maj. Gen. John A.

Drum, Lt. Gen. Hugh A., led the First Army in WWII.

Du Quesne, Marquis de Menneville, Governor of New France.

Forrest, Gen. Nathan B., Confederate Army, 1821-1877, cavalry officer.

Early, Gen. Jubal, Confederate Army, 1816-1894, led raid on Washington in Civil War.

Eglin, Lt. Col. Frederick, killed in a 1937 air crash.

Elmendorf, Hugh M.

Eustis, Brevet Brig. Gen. Abraham, artillery officer.

Fitzsimons, 1st Lt. William T., MD, the first American officer killed in action during WWI.

Franklin, Benjamin, 1706-1790, statesman.

Gates, Gen Horatio, 1728-1806, commanded army at Saratoga.

George, Brig. Gen. Harold S., WWI flier, died in 1942 air crash.

Goodfellow, Lt. John J., killed in action, WWI.

Gordon, Lt. Gen. John B., Condederate Army.

Grant, Gen. Ulysses S., 1822-1885, Civil War leader; U.S. President.

Greene, Gen. Nathaniel, 1742-1786, defeated the British in Southern campaigns during Revolutionary War.

Hamilton, Alexander, 1757-1804, first Secretary of The Treasury.

Hancock, John, signer of Declaration of Independence. Also, Gen. W.S. Hancock, served in the Civil War.

Hanscom, Laurence G., died in a 1941 air crash.

Harrison, William H., 1773-1341, President of the United States. Also Benjamin Harrison, 1833-1901, U.S. President.

Henry, Patrick, 1736-1799, statesman and patriot.

Hickam, Lt. Col. Horace M., died in a 1934 air crash.

Hill, Maj. Ployer P., killed in a 1935 air crash.

Hood, Gen. John B., Confederate Army.

Hooker, Gen. Joseph, 1814-1879, distinguished officer in Mexican and Civil Wars.

Houston, Sam, 1793-1863, a leader in the struggle to win control of Texas from Mexico. President of the Republic of Texas.

Irwin, Maj. Gen. George L., commanded the 57th Field Army Brigade, WWI.

Jackson, Andrew Jackson, President of the United States. Also Thomas "Stonewall" Jackson, 1814-1863, Confederate Army-- Shenandoah Valley Campaign.

Jefferson, Thomas, 1743-1825, U.S. President.

Johnson, Lt. Seymour, killed an a 1941 air crash.

Johnston, Gen. Joseph E., 1807-1891, Confederate Army.

Keesler, 2nd Lt. Samuel, Jr., killed in action, WWI.

Kelly, 2nd Lt. George E. M., first person to be killed flying in a military aircraft.

Kirtland, Col. Roy C., military aviation pioneer.

Knox, Maj. Gen. Henry, Chief of Artillery, Continental Army.

Lackland, Brig. Gen. Frank.

La Fayette, Marquis de, 1757-1834, who served under George Washington.

Langley, Samuel P., aviation pioneer.

Laughlin, 1st Lt. Jack, killed in action, WWII.

Leavenworth, Col. Henry, built Cantonment Leavenworth.

Lee, Gen. Robert E. Lee, 1807-1870, Confederate Army. Was defeated at Gettysburg.

Lewis, Capt. Meriwether, leader of the Lewis-Clark Expedition.

Lincoln, Abraham, 1809-1865, President of U.S.

Logan, Gen. J.A., 1826-1886, served in Civil War.

Loudon, Earl of, a general in the French & Indian War.

Lowry, 1st Lt. Francis B. Lowry, killed in WWII.

Luke, Lt. Frank, Jr., awarded Medal of Honor in WWI.

MacDill, Col. Leslie.

Madison, James, President of the United States.

March, Lt. Peyton C., killed in a 1918 air crash.

Marion, Frank, 1733-1795, led guerillas in South Carolina during Revolutionary War.

Mather, 2nd Lt. Carl, killed in a 1918 air crash.

Maxwell, 2nd Lt. William C., killed in a 1922 air crash.

McChord, Col. William, killed in a 1927 air crash.

McClellan: Maj. Gen. George B. McClellan, 1826-1885, General in Chief of U.S. Army in 1861-1862. Also Maj. Hezekiah McClellan, an pioneer of Alaskan aviation who was killed in an air crash.

McNair, Lt. Gen. Leslie J., commanded army ground forces. Killed in action, 1944.

McPherson, Maj. Gen. James B., killed in action during the Civil War.

Meade, Maj. Gen. George Meade, 1815-1872, commanded the Union forces at Gettysburg.

Monroe, James, President of the United States.

Montgomery, Gen. Richard, a Revolutionary War hero.

Moody, Maj. George P., killed in a 1941 air crash.

Morgan, Col. Daniel, 1736-1802, victorious at Cowpens.

Myer, Brig. Gen. Albert J., the first head of the Signal Corps.

Norton, Capt. Leland F., killed flying a mission over France, 1944.

Offutt, 1st Lt. Jarvis J., killed in a WWI air crash.

Ord, Maj. Gen. Edward, served in Civil War.

Peterson, 1st Lt. Edward J. Peterson, killed in a 1942 air crash.

Pickett, Gen. George E., 1825-1875, Confederate Army. Fought in the battle of Gettysburg.

Pitt, William, 1708-1778.

Polk, Gen. Leonidas, Confederate Army.

Pope, 1st Lt. Harley H., killed in a 1917 air crash.

Randolph, Capt. William M., killed in a 1930 air crash.

Reed, Maj. Walter, found a cure for Yellow Fever. Died 1902.

Reno, Gen. J. L., killed in action, Civil War.

Richardson, Brig. Wilds R., Alaskan explorer.

Riley, Maj. Gen. Bennett, a hero of the Mexican War.

Ritchie, Albert C., Governor of Maryland in 1926.

Rucker, Gen. Edmund W., Confederate Army.

Schuyler, Gen. Philip, Revolutionary War commander.

Scott: Gen. Winfield Scott, 1786-1866, hero of the War of 1812. Also, Cpl. Frank S. Scott, killed in a 1912 air crash.

Seward, William H., Secretary of State, purchased Alaska from Russia in 1867 for $7.2-million.

Shaw, 1st Lt. Ervin D., killed in action during WWI.

Shelby, Isaac, 1750-1826, Revolutionary War commander, also first Governor of Kentucky.

Sheridan, Lt. Gen. Philip H., 1831-1888, cavalry officer who commanded the Army of the Shenandoah.

Sherman, Gen. William T., 1820-1891, Civil War commander.

Sill, Brig. Gen. Joshua, killed in action during Civil War.

Standish, Capt. Miles, 1584-1656, military advisor to the Pilgrims.

Stewart, Brig. Gen. Daniel, of Revolutionary War.

Taylor, Zachary, 1704-1850, U.S. President.

Thomas, Gen. George H., 1816-1870, served in Civil War.

Tinker, Maj. Gen. Clarence L., killed in action, WWII.

Travis, Lt. Col. William B., a hero of The Alamo.

Tripler, Brevet Brig. Gen. Charles S., MD, served in Civil War.

Tryon, William, colonial Governor of North Carolina, and later of New York.

Tyler, John, President of the United States.

Tyndall, Lt. Frank B., killed in a 1930 air crash.

Warner Robins, Brig. Gen. Augustine, was head of Army Air Corps Materiel Division in WWII.

Warren: Francis E. Warren, recipient of Medal of Honor, and first Governor of Wyoming. Also, Gen. George J. Warren, hero of Bunker Hill.

Washington, George, 1732-1799, commanded Continental Army, also First President of United States.

Wayne, Gen. Anthony, 1745-1796, victor over the Indians at the Fallen Timbers, 1794.

Wheeler, Maj. Sheldon H., killed in a 1921 air crash.

Williams, 1st. Lt., Charles L., killed in a 1927 air crash.

Wood, Maj. Gen. Leonard, recipient of Medal of Honor in 1886 Indian Wars.

Wright-Patterson: Wilbur and Orville Wright, aviation pioneers. Also, Lt. Frank Patterson, killed in a 1931 air crash.

An unknown officer, circa 1870, wears a Cavalry pattern sword in this formal studio photo portrait.

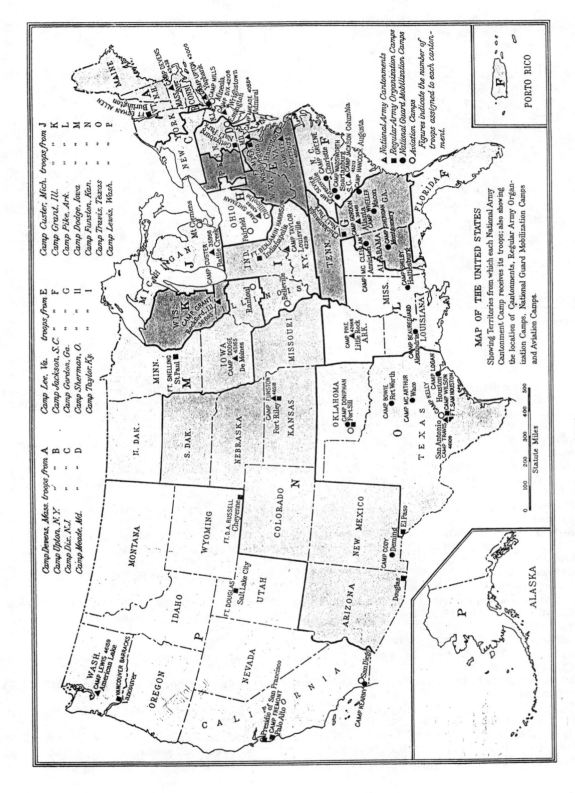

Army training and defense installations during WWI.

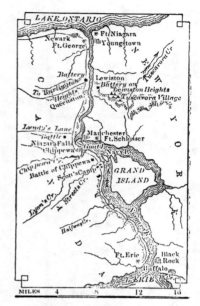

THE NIAGARA FRONTIER, 1812.

SCENE OF OPERATIONS IN THE SOUTH, 1780, 81.

Map Sources

When attempting to pin down the specific map locations of old military installations, you will find it useful to arm yourself with types of maps that have proven helpful aids. There are many types and sources of maps, and we found those below to offer maps that were especially good. You might wish to check directly with each source for information regarding availability and pricing. The addresses given appear to have been correct at publication time, but are subject to change.

De Lorme Mapping Company, P.O. Box 298, Freeport, ME 04032. Highly detailed atlas/gazetteer directories for ME, NH, NY, VT, PA, OH, MI, FL, CA, WA, and WI. Show back roads, abandoned railroads, trails, etc.

Historic Reprints, 3918 Leland Road, Louisville, KY 40207. Reprints of old city and county maps.

Hubbard, P.O. Box 104, Northbrook, IL 60062. Hard-plastic topographic relief maps of most mountainous areas of the U.S. are extremely detailed as to roads, trails, etc.

Library of Congress, Washington, DC 20540. Has old military maps.

National Archives, U.S. General Services Administration, Washington, DC 20408. Has old military maps.

National Cartographic Information Center, 507 National Center, 12201 Sunrise Valley Drive, Reston, VA 22092. Offers information on maps available from the U.S. Government.

National Ocean Survey, Riverside, MD 20737. Maps relating to the Civil War.

Nystrom, 3333 Elston Avenue, Chicago, IL 60618. Wall maps of the U.S. as it was during various wars.

Superintendent of Documents, Government Printing Office, Washington, DC 20402. Military maps.

Tennessee Valley Authority, Mapping Services Bureau, 400 West Summit Hill Drive (WPA3), Knoxville, TN 37902. Civil war maps.

U.S. Geological Survey, Map Distribution, Federal Center, Building 41, Box 25286, Denver, CO 80225. Maps of National Parks and other federal areas. Also, detailed 7.5-minutes (1:24000 scale) maps of all areas of the U.S.

Fort Sam Houston, Texas, as it appeared during WWI.

Left: A Spanish–American War soldier and his rifle. Right: A photo from the Indian War era shows a solder at Camp Alger wearing a New York beltplate.

Camps, Forts, Barracks, etc.	Where Situated
A. A. Humphries, Camp, VA	Became Ft. Belvoir
Abagadusset, Fort, ME	Near mouth of Kennebec River.
Abbott, Battery, ME	On Cow Island.
Abbott, Fort, VA	On Appomattox River, near City Point.
Abercrombie, Fort, ND	2 mi. below Grahams Pt. on Red River.
Aberdeen Proving Ground, MD	NW of Baltimore.
Abilene AAF, TX	WSW of Abilene.
Abraham Lincoln, Fort, ND	Near Bismarck. Ex-Ft. McKean.
Accotink, fortifications at, VA	
Acker, Battery, ME	At Fort McKinley.
Adacs Mission, Fort, TX	15 mi. W of Nacogdoches.
Adair, Battery, FL	At Ft. Taylor.
Adam Carson's Fort, PA	Clinton County.
Adams, Cantonment, MO	Near Jefferson Barracks.
Adams, Fort, AK	On Yukon River.
Adams, Fort, MA	Boston Harbor, became Ft. Independence.
Adams, Fort, OH	On St. Marys River, 25 mi. N of Fort Recovery.
Adams, Fort, RI	Brentons Point, Newport.
Adams, T.R., Fort, FL	On Caloosahatchee River.
Adams, Jack, Battery, MA	(see Jack Adams)
Adams Point, fort at, OR	On Columbia River. Became Ft. Stevens.
Adams Gen. Hospital, TN	Memphis.
Adams, Alva, Camp, CO	Denver
Adjacento Field, Brazil	Fortaleza.
Adobe, Fort, NM	200 mi. E of Ft. Bascom.
Advance, Camp, VA	Near Centerville.
Advance Towers, Fort, FL	Near Key West.
Aiken AAF, SC	NNE of Aiken.
Ainsworth AAF, NE	WNW of Ainsworth.
Ajo AAF, AZ	Childs.
Alabama, Fort, AL	Coosa River, Elmore County.
Alabama, Fort, FL	Hillsboro River, 25 mi. from Tampa Bay.
Alachua AAF, FL	NE of Gainesville.
Alamo, Fort, TX	San Antonio.
Alamogordo AAF, NM	SW of Alamogordo.
Albany Field, GA	SW of Albany.
Albany, Fort, NY	Hudson River, near Albany.
Albany, Fort, VA	Alexandria County.
Albert C. Ritchie, Camp, MD	Became Ft. Ritchie.
Albrook Field, Panama	SE side Panama Canal.
Albuquerque Aux. AAF, NM	SW of Albuquerque.
Alburgh Springs, fort at, VT	Grand Isle County.
Alburtis, Battery, DE	At Ft. Delaware.
Alcatraz Island, fortifications on, CA	San Francisco harbor.
Alderton Point, battery at, MA	
Alert, Camp, CA	Near San Francisco.
Alert, Camp, KS	Became Ft. Larned.
Alexander, Fort, AK	Bristol Bay.
Alexander, Battery, CA	At Ft. Baker.
Alexander, Battery, MD	Near Washington.

Alexander, Fort, MD	3 mi. N of Georgetown, DC. Became Redoubt Davis.
Alexander, Fort, MT	Yellowstone River at mouth of Rosebud.
Alexander, Fort, VA	Petersburg.
Alexander Hayes, Fort, VA	Petersburg.
Alexandria AAF, LA	WNW of Alexandria.
Alexandria, Fort, AL	Near Mobile.
Alexandria National Cemetery, LA	Pineville.
Alexandria National Cemetery, VA	Alexandria.
Alexis, Fort, AL	Near Mobile.
Alfred Vail, Camp, NJ	Became Ft. Monmouth.
Alger, Camp, GA	Chickamauga Park.
Alger, Camp, VA	Near Dunn Loring.
Algernon, Fort, VA	Old Point Comfort.
Alibamo, Fort, MS	Yazoo River.
Allatoona Pass, fort at, GA	Allatoona Pass.
Alleghany, Camp, WV	Pocahontas County.
Allegheny, Fort, VA	On Beverly & Staunton Turnpike.
Allegheny Arsenal, PA	Pittsburgh.
Albin, Battery, DE	At Ft. Delaware.
Allen, Fort, PA	Lehigh River, near Weissport.
Allen's Fort, PA	Smith's Twp., Washington County.
Alliance AAF, NE	SE of Alliance.
Aloe AAF, TX	SW of Victoria.
Alpena Field, MI	W of Alpena.
Alton Prison, IL	Alton.
Altona, Fort, DE	Near Wilmington.
Altus AAF, OK	NE of Altus.
Alva Adams, Camp, CO	Denver.
Alven, Fort, NY	In Cherry Valley.
Alvin Sanders, Camp, NE	Lincoln.
Alvord, Camp, OR	Grant County.
Amanda, Fort, OH	Auglaize River, 60 mi. SE Ft. Wayne, IN.
Amboy Flying Camp, NJ	Perth Amboy.
Amelia Island, forts on, FL	Forts Clinch & St. George.
Amity, Fort, LA	Amite City.
Ammen, Fort, TN	Loudon.
Amory, Fort, NC	New Bern.
Amsterdam, Fort, NY	New York City.
Anahuac, Fort, TX	Chambers County.
Anastasia Island, forts on, FL	Forts Matanzas & Preston.
Anchusa, Fort, FL	Entrance of Pensacola Bay.
Ancient, Fort, OH	Miami River, Warren County.
Andaraque, Fort, NY	Lake Champlain.
Anderson, Battery, VT	Bermuda Hundred.
Anderson, Battery, VA	Ft. Monroe.
Anderson, Camp/Fort, CA	Humboldt County.
Anderson, Fort, KY	Paducah.
Anderson, Fort, NC	New Bern (site of old Ft. St. Philip).
Anderson, Fort, VA	Petersburg.
Anderson, J.W., Camp, CA	Sacramento.
Andersonville Nat'l. Cemetery, GA	Andersonville.
Andersonville Prison, GA	Andersonville.
Andreavsky, Fort, AK	Yukon River.
Andrew, Fort, MA	Gurnet Point, 9 mi. NE Plymouth.

Andrew, Camp, VA   Alexandria.
Andrew Johnson, Camp, KY   Barboursville.
Andrews, Fort, FL   Apalachee Bay.
Andrews, Fort, MA   Peddocks Island.
Androscoggin, Fort, ME   Androscoggin River.
Angel Island, fort on, CA   Became Ft. McDowell.
Anill, Fort, NY   New York City.
Ann, Fort, FL   Indian River.
Ann, Fort, NY   On Wood Creek, Washington County.
Annapolis, fortifications at, MD   Forts Horn, Madison, & Severn, & USNA
Annapolis National Cemetery, MD   Annapolis.
Anne, Fort, RI   Goat Island, Newport.
Anne Run, Fort, ME   Castine.
Anniston AAF, AL   SW of Anniston.
Annutteeliga, Fort, FL   Brooksville.
Antes, Fort, PA   Lycoming County.
Anthony Nose, works at, NY
Antietam National Cemetery, MD   Sharpsburg.
Apache, Fort, AZ   White Mtn. River; ex-Camp Ord.
Apalachicola AAF, FL   W of Apalachicola.
Apalachicola Arsenal, FL   Apalachicola River.
Apalachicola, Fort, FL   "
Appleby's Fort, PA   Kittanning.
Apple River, Fort, IL   Elizabeth.
Aquia Creek, forts at, VA   Potomac River.
Arbuckle, Camp, I.T. (OK)   On Red Fork of Canadian.
Arbuckle, Camp, WV   Lewisburg.
Arbuckle, Fort, FL   Lake Ishtopoga.
Arbuckle, Fort, I.T. (OK)   Washita River, Chichasaw Nation.
Archangel Gabriel, Fort, AK   Baranoff Island.
Archangel Michael, Fort. AK   "
Ardmore AAF, OK   NE of Berwyn.
Argyle, Fort, GA   Savannah.
Arivaypa, Fort, AZ   Pinal County; became Ft. Breckinridge.
Arkansas Post, fort at, AR   Arkansas River; Ft. Hindman.
Arkokisa, Fort, TX   Trinity River.
Arlington National Cemetery, VA   Opposite Washington, DC.
Armistead, Fort, FL   Sarasota.
Armistead, Fort, MD   Hawkins Point, Patapsco River.
Armistead, Fort, TN   Monroe County.
Armory Sq. Gen. Hospital, DC   Washington.
Armstrong, Fort, AL   Etowah River, near the Coosa.
Armstrong, Fort, FL   At Dade's battle ground.
Armstrong, Fort, FL   Manatee River.
Armstrong, Fort, IL   Rock Island, became Rock Isl. Arsenal.
Armstrong, Fort, PA   Kittanning.
Army & Navy Gen. Hospital, AR   Hot Springs.
Arnold Battery, NJ   At Ft. Mott.
Arnold, Camp, RI   Pawtucket.
Arnold, Fort, NY   West Point.
Arrowsic Island, fort on, ME   Hammond's Fort.
Arruinado, Fort, FL   Pensacola Bay.
Ascension Field, Ascension Isl.   Atlantic Ocean.
Ash Barracks, TN   Nashville.

Ashby's Fort, WV	Frankfort.
Ashcroft's Fort, PA	Fayette County.
Ashepoo Redoubt, SC	Colleton County.
Ashley, Fort, UT	Utah Lake.
Ashs Point, Fort, ME	Near Goldsboro.
Assinniobine, Fort, MT	On Beaver Creek, Choteau Co.
Assumption, Fort, IL	Ohio River, Massac Co.
Assumption, Fort, TN	Memphis
Astoria, battery at, NY	Astoria, Queens Co.
Astoria, fort at, OR	Ft. George.
Asylum Gen. Hospital, TN	Knoxville.
Atcheson, Camp., ND	Devils Lake, Ramsey Co.
Atkinson, Camp, FL	Suwanee River.
Atkinson, Camp, GA	Atlanta.
Atkinson, Camp, LA	Lake Charles.
Atkinson, Camp, WV	Charleston.
Atkinson Field, British Guiana	Georgetown.
Atkinson, Fort, IA	Turkey River, Winneshiek Co.
Atkinson, Fort, KS	Arkansas River, Ford Co.
Atkinson, Fort, NE	Near Council Bluffs.
Atkinson, Fort, WI	Rock River, head of Lk. Koshkonong.
Atterbury AAF, IN	N of Columbus.
Aubrey, Fort, KS	Arkansas River.
Au Fer, Fort, NY	Lake Champlain.
Augur Gen. Hospital, VA	Alexandria.
Augur, Camp, NE	Omaha.
Augur, Camp, WY	Little Wood River, became Ft. Washakie.
Augusta Arsenal, GA	Augusta.
Augusta Arsenal, ME	Augusta.
Augusta, Fort, GA	Augusta.
Augusta, fort at, ME	Augusta.
Augusta, Fort, PA	Sunbury.
Augustin Battery, MD	At Ft. Carroll.
Aurenea, Fort, NY	Albany.
Austin Arsenal, TX	Austin.
Avon Park AAF, FL	NW of Avon Park.
Ayres Battery, NY	At Ft. Wadsworth.

Gen. Winfield Scott

"Stonewall" Jackson, CSA

At an outdoor control tower, during WWII,
flight trainees get ready to head into the
wild blue yonder.

Babbitt, Camp. CA	Visalia.
Babbitt Island Reservation, FL	St. Johns River.
Backus Battry, GA	At Ft. Screven.
Bacon, J.M., Camp, MN	Walker.
Bacon Race Church, Fort, VA	Occoquan River.
Badlam's Battery, NY	New York City.
Badlands, Camp, ND	W bank of Little Missouri River.
Bagley Battery, NC	At Ft. Caswell.
Bahia, Fort, TX	Bahia.
Bailey Battery, AL	Near Mobile.
Bailey Battery, MD	4 mi. N of Georgetown, DC.
Bailey's Island, garrison on, ME	Harpswell.
Bainbridge AAF, GA	W of Lynn.
Bainbridge, Fort, AL	17 mi. SE of Tuskegee.
Baker Battery, NY	At Ft. Totten.
Baker, Camp, MD	On lower Potomac River.
Baker, Camp, MT	Became Ft. Logan.
Baker, Fort, CA	Mud River, Humboldt County.
Baker, Fort, CA	Line Point, San Francisco Harbor.
Baker, Fort, DC	On Eastern Branch, near Washington.
Baker, Fort, NM	Manzano.
Baker, Fort, VA	Near Chain Bridge; became Ft. Ethan Allen
Baker, Fort, WV	Ohio River at Cresaps Bottom.
Baker's Blockhouse, VT	Ft. Frederick
Balboa Fill Landing Strip, Panama	Became Albrook Field.
Baldwin, Camp/Fort, VA	
Balfour, Fort, SC	Pocotaligo.
Balfour Gen. Hospital, VA	Portsmouth.
Baldwin Battery, CA	At Ft. Winfield Scott.
Balize Battery, LA	Mouth of Mississippi River.
Ball, Fort, OH	Sandusky River, opp. Tiffin.
Balls Bluff National Cemetery, VA	Potomac River.
Balls Landing Battery, TN	Cumberland River.
Ball, Tom, Camp, TX	Houston.
Bangs Island, fort on, ME	A/k/a Cushings Isl. & Fort Isl.
Bankhead, Fort, FL	Key Biscayne, FL.
Bankhead, Fort, MO	New Madrid.
Banks, Camp, LA	Baton Rouge.
Banks, Fort, MA	Grovers Cliff, near Boston.
Banning, Camp, CA	San Bernardino.
Barbee, Fort, OH	St. Marys.
Barbette Battery, NY	New York City.
Barbour Battery, NY	At Ft. Wadsworth.
Barbour, Fort, FL	Apalachee River, near Aspalaga.
Barbour, Fort, VA	Norfolk.
Barclay, Camp, DC	Columbia College.
Barker, Fort, FL	Esteinhatchee River.
Barksdale Field, LA	Near Shreveport.
Barlow Battery, NY	At Ft. H. G. Wright.
Barnard, Fort, VA	5 mi. SW of Washington, DC.
Barnes Gen. Hospital, DC	Soldiers' Home.
Barnum, Fort, GA	Near Okeefinokee Swamp.

Barnwell AAF, GA	NW of Barnwell.
Barnwell, Fort, FL	Near mouth of St. Johns River.
Barnwell, Fort, NC	Craven County.
Barr's Fort, PA	In the Derry Settlement.
Barrancas, Fort, FL	Near Pensacola.
Barrancas National Cemetery, FL	N side Pensacola Bay.
Barrel Point, battery at, VA	
Barren Hill, Post, PA	Philadelphia.
Barret, Camp, CA	Fruitvale.
Barrett, Fort, AZ	At the Pimas Villages.
Barrington, Fort, GA	Altanaha River, McIntosh County.
Barry, Camp, DC	Near Bladensburg tollgate.
Barry Battery, NY	At Ft. Wadsworth.
Bartlett Battery, MA	At Ft. Warren.
Bartletts Point, battery at, NY	French Creek.
Barton Battery, GA	Savannah.
Barton Battery, MA	At Ft. Rodman.
Barton Battery, SC	Near Ft. Wagner.
Bartow AAF, FL	NE of Bartow.
Bartow, Camp, WV	8 mi. from Greenbrier River.
Bartow, Fort, NC	Roanoke Island.
Bartow, Fort, NM	Canadian River, San Miguel County.
Basinger Battery, MA	At Ft. Strong.
Basley, Fort, PA	
Bastion Bay Reservation, LA	
Bateman, Camp, KS	Near Ft. Leavenworth.
Bates Battery, KY	Covington.
Bates, Camp, MD	Near Poolesville.
Bates Field, AL	ENE of Mobile.
Baton Rouge Barracks, LA	Baton Rouge.
Baton Rouge National Cemetery, LA	"
Battelle des Illinois, Camp, IN	A/k/a Ft. Harrison.
Batterskill, camp on the, NY	
Battery Park, VT	See Burlington.
Battery Point, Camp, DE	Near Delaware City.
Battle Creek, Camp, UT	Near Salt Lake City.
Battle Ground National Cemetery, DC	Near Soldiers' Home.
Baxter Gen. Hospital, VT	Burlington.
Bayard, Fort, DC	Near Tennallytown.
Bayard, Fort, NM	Pinos Altos, Grant County.
Bayards Hill, battery at, NY	New York City.
Bayon, Fort, MS	Jackson County.
Bayon Sauvages Battery, LA	
Bayou Teche, fortifications at, LA	
Bay Point, Fort, SC	Phillips Island.
Bayside Reservation, NJ	Near Pt. Comfort, Monmouth County.
Beach Bottom, blockhouse at, WV	
Beacon Island Reservation, NC	Mouth of Ocracoke Inlet.
Beale, Camp, CA	
Beale Field, CA	10 mi. W of Marysville.
Beale's Springs, Camp, AZ	43 mi. E of Ft. Mojave.
Beaufort, Fort, NC	Topsail Inlet, 15 mi. from Wilmington.
Beaufort National Cemetery, SC	Beaufort

Beaubarnois, Fort, MN	On Lake Pepin.
Beaulien, Fort, GA	Savannah.
Beaumonts Point, fort at, MD	Severn River, near Annapolis.
Beauregard, Camp, MS	Vicksburg.
Beauregard, Fort, KY	Columbus.
Beauregard, Fort, LA	Harrisburg.
Beauregard, Fort, TN	
Beauregard, Fort, VA	Leesburg.
Beauregard, Fort #1, SC	Bay Point, Sullivans Isl.
Beauregard, Fort #2, SC	Phillips Isl., near Port Royal.
Beaver, blockhouse at, PA	Beaver Creek.
Beaver Canyon, fort at, UT	Near Beaver City; Ft. Cameron.
Beckets Fort, PA	Monongahela River, Washington County.
Beckwith, Camp, VA	Lewinsville.
Beale Fld., CA	10 mi. W of Marysville.
Bedford AAF, MA	E of Concord.
Bedford, Fort, PA	Raystown.
Bedloes Isl., fort on, NY	Became Ft. Wood, NY City harbor.
Bee Battery, SC	Sullivans Isl.
Beecher Battery, NY	At Ft. Schuyler.
Beecher, Camp, KS	Near mouth of Little Arkansas River (ex-Camp Davidson).
Beech Grove, fort at, KY	Cumberland River, Laurel County.
Beef Hill, Fort, MA	Boston harbor.
Beekmans Slip, redoubt at, NY	lower Manhattan, NY City.
Boeman's blockhouse, PA	Near Wheeling Creek.
Beeson's blockhouse, PA	Uniontown.
Beetor's Fort, PA	Washington County.
Beggs, Fort, IL	DuPage River, at Plainfield.
Belknap, Fort, MT	Yellowstone River.
Belknap, Fort, TX	Red Fork of Brazos River.
Bell, Battery, NY	At Ft. Schuyler.
Belle Chasse Aux. Field #15514, LA	SW of Belle Chasse.
Belle Fontaine Barracks, MO	5 mi. from mouth of Missouri River.
Belle Plain, Camp, MN	At Yellow Medicine Agency.
Belleville, Fort, WV	
Bellevue Rifle Range, NE	Missouri River, 18 mi. from Omaha.
Bellingham, Fort, WA	On Bellingham Bay.
Bellona Arsenal, VA	Near Richmond.
Belmont, fortifications at, MO	Missisippi River.
Belvoir, Fort, VA	Belvoir.
Bemis Heights, fortifications at, NY	Hudson River, near Stillwater.
Benedict Field, VI	
Bender, Fort, NY	Rochester.
Benicia Arsenal & Barracks, CA	Benicia.
Benjamin Battery, NY	At Ft. Michie.
Benjamin Harrison, Fort, IN	E of Indianapolis.
Bennett, Camp, SC	Hilton Head.
Bennett, Fort, SD	Missouri River, at Cheyenne Agency.
Bennett, Fort, VA	Potomac River, ½-mi. N of Georgetown.
Bennett's Tavern, blockhouse at, PA	Crawford County.
Benning, Camp/Fort, GA	Columbus.
Benson Battery, MD	Near Tenallytown, DC.
Benton Barracks, MO	St. Louis.
Benton, Camp, MD	Poolesville.

Benton, Fort, CO	Choteau County.
Bent's Fort, CO	Arkansas River, Bent County.
Bergen Heights, fort at, NJ	
Bergstrom AAF, TX	Austin.
Bermuda Hundred, forts at, VA	James River.
Berry Battery, ME	At Ft. McKinley.
Berry, Camp, ME	Near Portland.
Berry, Fort, VA	4 mi. from Washington, DC.
Berthold, Fort, ND	Missouri River, McLean County, 30 mi. below mouth of Little Missouri River.
Berwick, Fort, LA	Near Brashear City.
Berwick, fortifications at, ME	
Bethlehem, stockade at, PA	
Beverly National Cemetery, NJ	Beverly.
Beversrede, Fort, PA	At mouth of Schuylkill River.
Bibb, Fort, AL	Butler County.
Biddeford, fortifications at, ME	
Biddle, Camp, PA	Carlisle.
Bidwell, Fort, CA	In Surprise Valley, Modoc Valley.
Bienvenue Battery, LA	On rt. bank of Bayou Bienvenue.
Big Beaver Creek, fort at, VA	Fayette County.
Big Bend, camp at, OR	Rogue River.
Big Bottom, fort at, OH	Muskingum River, Morgan County.
Big Cheyenne Agency, fort at, ND	Missouri River; Ft. Berthold.
Big Cottonwood Creek, camp on, SD	60 mi. SW of Pierre.
Big Cypress Swamp, forts in, FL	Everglades area.
Bigelow Battery, FL	At Ft. Dade.
Biggin Bridge Redoubt, SC	Near Monks Corner.
Biggs Field, TX	NE of El Paso.
Big Horn Barracks, MT	Became Ft. Custer.
Big Spring AAF, TX	SW of Big Spring.
Big Stone Lake, camp on, MN	Temporary camp in 1860.
Big Tybee Isl., batteries on, GA	Near Savannah.
Billings, Fort, NJ	Opp. Ft. Mifflin, PA.
Biloxi, Fort, MS	E side of Bay of Biloxi.
Bingham Battery, SC	At Ft. Moultrie.
Bingham's Fort, PA	In Tuscarora Vly., Juniata County.
Bird, Fort, PA (a/k/a Ft. Burd)	Monongahelia River.
Birds Island, Battery on, GA	Savannah River; Battery Hamilton.
Birds Point, fortifications on, MO	Opp. Cairo, IL.
Bishop AAF, CA	ENE of Bishop.
Bishop, Fort, KY	Louisa.
Bishop, Fort, LA	Pattersonville.
Bitter Cottonwood, Camp, NE	22 mi. W of Ft. Laramie.
Black, Camp, NY	Hempstead.
Black, Fort, OH	10 mi. from Greenville.
Black, Fort, WV	Abingdon.
Black Canyon Creek, Camp, OR	Temporary camp in 1859.
Blackmore, Fort, VA	Scott County.
Black Isl., fort on, IL	1 mi. above mouth of Ohio River.
Black Point, fort at, ME	Ft. Scarborough.
Black Rock, fort at, NY	Buffalo, became Ft. Porter.
Blackstone AAF, VA	N of Camp Pickett.
Blackwells Isl., fort on, NY	Ft. Maxey.
Blair Battery, ME	At Ft. Williams.

Blair, Camp, SC	Near Charleston.
Blair, Fort, KS	Baxter Springs.
Blaisdell. Fort, VA	Petersburg.
Blake, Camp, NM	Near Ft. Thorn.
Blake, Camp, TX	Rio San Pedro.
Blakely, Fort, AL	Near Mobile.
Blanchard, Fort, NC	Roanoke Isl., became Ft. Parke.
Blanding, Camp, FL	E of Starke.
Blaney Battery, CA	At Ft. Winfield Scott.
Blantons Hill, Fort, KY	Frankfort.
Bledsoe's Fort, TN	Near Gallatin.
Blenker, Fort, VA	Became Ft. Reynolds.
Bliss, Fort, TX (first)	Rio Grande, near Franklin.
Bliss, Fort, TX (second)	El Paso.
Blockhouse Point, blockhouse at, NY	
Bloomingdale, Fort, NY	Bloomingdale.
Bluethenthal Field, NC	NE of Wilmington.
Bluff, Fort, AL	Morgan County.
Bluie West-1 Field (BW-1), Greenland	Narsarssuak.
Blunt, Fort. I.T. (OK)	Near Ft. Gibson.
Bluthe's Point, fort at, SC	Ft. Winyaw.
Blythe AAF, CA	WNW of Blythe.
Blythe, Camp, MS	Near Corinth.
Blytheville AAF, AR	NW of Blytheville.
Boca Raton AAF, FL	NW of Boca Raton.
Boggs, Fort, GA	Near Savannah.
Bogue Point, fort at, SC	Bogue Isl.; Ft. Macon.
Bois Blanc Isl. Reservation, MI	Detroit River.
Boise Barracks/Fort, ID (first)	Boise City.
Boise Fort, ID (second)	Snake River.
Bolivar, fort or stockade at, OH	
Bolivar Heights, fort at, WV	Near Harpers Ferry.
Bolivar Point, fort at, TX	Became Ft. Travis, Galveston Bay.
Bolling Field, DC	Anacostia.
Bomford Battery, PA	At Ft. Monroe.
Bomford, Camp, NC	Raleigh.
Bon Homme, Fort, IL	Illinois River.
Bonnett's Fort, WV	Wheeling.
Bon Secours, Fort, MN	On Lake Pepin.
Boomer Battery, MS	Vicksburg.
Boone, Camp/Fort, TN	Clarksville.
Boone, Fort, KY	Boonesboro.
Boone, Fort, PA	On Muddy Run, Northumberland County.
Boonville Battery, MO	8 mi. below Boonville, on the bluffs.
Boquet's Redout, PA	Pittsburgh.
Bordentown, cantonment at, NJ	
Boreman, fort at, WV	Parkersburg.
Borinquen Field, PR	
Boscawen, fort at, NH	
Bosley, Fort, PA	Washington.
Boswick, blockhouses at, NY	Long Island.
Botany Bay Isl., fort at, NC	North Edisto.
Bourbon, Fort, LA	Miss. River, below New Orleans.
Boush's Bluff, fort at, VA	Sewells Point.
Boutelle Battery, CA	At Ft. Winfield Scott.

Bowdoin Battery, ME	At Ft. Lovett, Cushings Isl.
Bowen Field, Haiti	Port au Prince.
Bowie, Camp, TX	Ft. Worth.
Bowie, Fort, AZ	Apache Pass.
Bowman Field, KY	Louisville.
Bowyer Battery, AL	At Ft. Morgan.
Bowyer, Fort, AL	On later site of Ft. Morgan.
Box, Fort, NY	Brooklyn.
Boyd, Camp, VA	Potomac River.
Boyds Creek, battery at, SC	
Boyds Island, blockhouse on, NY	
Boykin, Fort, VA	Richmond area.
Boyle, Fort, KY	Muldraugh's Hill, Marion County.
Boynton, Camp, GA	At Chickamauga Park.
Braden, Fort, FL	Ocklockonee River.
Bradford Battery, NY	At Ft. Terry.
Bradford, Camp, MD	Baltimore.
Bradford, Fort, MD	Hagerstown.
Bradley, Camp, TN	Murfreesboro.
Bradley Field, CT	Windsor Locks.
Brady, Fort, MI	Sault Ste. Marie.
Brady, Fort, PA	Muncy Creek, at Muncy.
Brady, Fort, VA	James River.
Bragg, Fort, CA	50 mi. S of Cape Mendocino.
Bragg, Fort, NC	Fayetteville.
Bragg, Fort, TN	Near Chattanooga.
Branch, Fort, IN	Gibson County.
Branch, Fort, NC	
Brandley Field	
Brandywine Creek, camp at, DE	
Brannon Redoubt, TN	Stone River.
Brazos Agency, camp at, TX	
Brazos Isl., fort on, TX	Ft. Polk.
Brazos River, fort on, TX	Ft. Phantom Hill.
Brazos Santiago, fort at, TX	Ft. Polk.
Breach Inlet, battery at, SC	Charleston Harbor.
Breckenridge, Camp, TN	Near TN/KY state line.
Breckinridge, Fort, AZ	Arivaipa & San Pedro Rivers; became Ft. Stanford.
Breeds Hill, fortifications on, MA	Near Boston.
Brent, Fort, CO	A/k/a Brent's Fort.
Brentons Point, fort at, RI	Ft. Adams.
Brewer, Camp, MS	Birmingham.
Brewington (Brewerton), fort, NY	On Lake Oneida.
Briar Creek, fort at, GA	
Bridewell Magazine, PA	Philadelphia.
Bridgeport AAF, CT	S of Stratford.
Bridger, Fort, WY	Near Carter's Station, Uinta County.
Bridgman's Fort, NH	Connecticut River at Hillsdale.
Briggs, Camp, ND	Fargo.
Brisbane, Camp, FL	St. John's County.
Briske Isle, fort at, PA	Presque Isle (apparently).
Broadnax, Fort, FL	Near the Chickuchatty.
Broad River, camp on, SC	Near Fish Dam Ford.
Broadway Barracks, NY	Manhattan, NY City.

Brooke Battery, LA	At Ft. St. Philip.
Brooke, Camp, VA	Newport News.
Brooke, Fort, FL	Head of Tampa Bay.
Brooke, Frank, Fort, FL	On Dead Man's Bay.
Brookfield, fort at, MA	
Brookley Field, AL	S of Mobile.
Brookline, Fort, MA	Near Boston.
Brooklyn Army Terminal, NY	Brooklyn.
Brooks Battery, VA	James River.
Brooks Field, TX	SE of San Antonio.
Brooks, Fort, FL	Ocklawaha River.
Brooksville AAF, FL	NW of Masarkytown.
Bross, Fort, VA	Petersburg.
Brothers Isls. Reservation, CA	San Francisco harbor.
Brough, Camp, OH	Near Gallipolis.
Brough, Camp, TN	Nashville.
Browder, Fort, AL	Barbour County.
Brown, Camp, FL	At Ft. Pickens.
Brown, Camp, WY	Became Ft. Washakie.
Brown, Fort, FL	St. John's River, 10 mi. S of Palatka.
Brown, Fort, GA	Near Savannah.
Brown, Fort, NY	Near Plattsburgh.
Brown, Fort, NC	Near New Bern.
Brown, Fort, OH	Auglaize River.
Brown, Fort, PA	Pittstown (see Ft. Ralston).
Brown, Fort, RI	On Narragansett Bay.
Brown, Fort, TX	Brownsville.
Brown Gen. Hospital, KY	Louisville.
Brown, Harvey, Battery, NY	See Harvey Brown.
Browning, Fort, MT	
Brownlow, Camp, KY	Piketon.
Brownsville National Cemetery, TX	Brownsville.
Bruce, Fort, TN	Clarksville.
Brumby Battery, GA	At Ft. Screven.
Bruning AAF, NE	E of Bruning.
Bryan AAF, TX	W of Bryan.
Bryant's plantation, batteries at, VA	Gloucester Point.
Buade, Fort, MI	Mackinac.
Buchanan Battery, NC	Near Ft. Fisher.
Buchanan, Camp/Fort, PR	S shore of San Juan Bay.
Buchanan, Camp, TX	San Antonio.
Buchanan, Fort, AZ	45 mi. SE of Tucson, ex-Camp Monroe.
Buchanan, Fort, LA	Brashear City.
Buchanan, Fort, WV	
Buckeye, Fort, FL	Esteinhatchee River.
Buckingham AAF, FL	E of city of Fort Myers.
Buckley Field, CO	E of Denver.
Buckner, Camp, KY	At Cumberland Ford.
Buckner, Fort, TN	Chattanooga.
Budds Ferry, battery at, MD	
Buell, Camp, KY	Parritsville.
Buena Vista, Fort, FL	St. John's River.
Buffalo Barracks, NY	Buffalo.
Buffalo, Camp, VA	Near Uptons Hill.
Buffalo, fort at, NY	Ft. Porter.

Buffalo, Fort, VA	Road from Falls Church to Washington.
Buffalo Springs Reservation, TX	Trinity River.
Buffington, Fort, GA	Cherokee County.
Buford, Camp, ID	Brunean River, near jct. with Snake Riv.
Buford, Camp, MD	Charles County.
Buford, Fort, ND	Near mouth of Yellowstone River.
Buford, John, Fort, WY	Became Ft. Sanders.
Bull, Camp, OH	
Bull, Fort, NY	Wood Creek, 2 mi. from Rome.
Bullocks Point, battery at, RI	Narragansett Bay.
Bulls Bay, fortifications at, SC	Near Charleston.
Bulls Ferry, blockhouse at, NY	North River, NY City.
Bulowville, fortifications at, FL	Tomaku, Musquito County.
Bunker Hill, fortifications at, MA	Near Charlestown.
Bunker Bill, Fort, DC	Washington, 2 mi. E of Soldiers' Home.
Bunker Hill, Fort, NY	NY City.
Buns Hill, battery at, NY	Near Ft. Constitution, West Point.
Burbank Battery, KY	Near Covington.
Burbank, Camp, KY	Warsaw.
Burbank, Camp, TX	Limpia River.
Burchsted Battery, FL	At Ft. Dade.
Burd, Fort, PA	Muncy.
Burdette, Camp, ME	Near Ft. Preble,
Burgess, Camp, KY	Bowling Green.
Burgess Field, PA	Uniontown.
Burgett's Fort, PA	Burgettstown.
Burgoyne, Camp, NY	Saratoga.
Burgwin Cantonment, NM	9 mi. N of Taos.
Burke Battery, NY	At Ft. Hamilton.
Burlington, cantonment at, NJ	
Burlington, fort at, VT (1812)	Later called Battery Park.
Burlington, reservation in, DE	
Burlings Slip, fort at, NY	NY City.
Burnet, Fort, NY	Oswego.
Burnett, Battery, KY	Near Covington.
Burnham Battery, CA	At Ft. Mason.
Burnside Battery, GA	Tybee Isl.
Burnside, Camp, KY	Lincoln County.
Burnside, Fort, NC	Roanoke Isl.
Burpee Battery, VA	James River, near Bermuda Hundred.
Burrows, Fort, ME	
Burton, Camp, CA	San Diego.
Burwell, Camp, TX	Eagle Pass.
Burwells Bay, fort at, VA	15 mi. from Norfolk.
Bushnell AAF, FL	E of Bushnell.
Bushnell Battery, TN	Chattanooga.
Bushnell, Camp, OH	Columbus.
Bute, Fort, LA	Miss. River, just below Baton Rouge.
Bute, Fort, NY	Near Ft. Stanwix, Rome.
Butler, Camp, IL	Springfield.
Butler, Camp, LA	Baton Rouge.
Butler, Camp, MI	Mount Clemens.
Butler, Camp, National Cemetery, IL	Springfield.
Butler, Fort, FL	St. John's River, opp. Volusia.

Butler, Fort, LA   Donaldsonville.
Butler, Fort, NC   Cherokee County.
Butler, Fort, NM   Gallinas River.
Butler, Fort, VA   Newport News.
Butlers Rock, battery at, ME   Mouth of Kennebunk River.
Butterfield Battery, NY   At Ft. H. G. Wright.
Butterfield, Camp, KS   Became Camp Beecher.
Buttonwood Blockhouse, PA   Hanover.
Butts Hill, fort at, RI   Newport.
Buzzards Bay, fortifications at, MA   See Elizabeth Island.
Buzzards Roost, fortifications at, GA
Byington, Fort, TN   Knoxville.
Byllings Point, fort at, NJ   See Billings & Billingsport.

C.A.P. Base #232, MD   N of Westminster.
Cacaphon Stockade, WV   Cacaphon Creek, Morgan County.
Cadwallader, Camp, DC   Kalorama Heights.
Cadwallader, Camp, PA   Philadelphia.
Cady, Camp, CA   Mojave River, 145 mi. NE of Los Angeles
Caffery, Camp, LA   Covington.
Cahaniaga, Fort, NY   A/k/a Ft. Caughnawaga.
Cahokia, fort at, IL   Miss. River, 4 mi. below St. Louis.
Cahunke, Fort, NC   40 mi. SW of Snowhill.
Cajon, Camp, CO   15 mi. from Cajon Pass.
Caldwell, Camp, DC   Washington.
Caldwell, fort at, NY   Ft. William Henry.
Calhoun, Fort, NE   Missouri River, 17 mi. above Omaha.
Calhoun, Fort, VA   Hampton Roads, became Ft. Wood.
Camp California, VA   Near Fairfax Court House.
Calif. State Soldiers' Home   Yountville.
Call, Camp, GA   Hall County.
Call, Fort, FL   Volusia.
Callahan's Ranch, camp near, CA   In Scotts Valley.
Callaways, Fort, MO   Warren County.
Calvert, Camp, KY   London.
Calvert, Camp, TN   London County.
Cambridge, star battery at, SC

Camden, battery at, ME
Cameron Battery, DC   1 mi. above Georgetown.
Cameron Battery, FL   Near Ft. Pickens.
Cameron, Camp, AZ   15 mi. NE of Tubac.
Cameron, Camp, MA   Near Boston.
Cameron, Camp, PA   Harrisburg.
Cameron, Fort, TN   Chattanooga.
Cameron, Fort, UT   Near Beaver City.
Cameron Station, VA   Alexandria.
Caminada Bay Reservation, FL
Cammaas Woods, camps at, PA   Near Philadelphia.
Campayne, Fort, IN   Delaware River.
Campbell AAF, KY   S of Hopkinsville.
Campbell, Camp, TN   Nashville.
Campbell, Fort, GA
Campbell, Fort, KY   Hopkinsville.
Campbell, Fort, NC   Near Wilmington.
Campbell, Fort, OH   Maumee Rapids.
Campbell, Fort, PA   Juniata County.
Campbells Blockhouse, PA   Washington County.
Campus Martins, Fort, OH   Marietta.
Canadian River, cantonment on, I.T. (OK) Near 100th meridian.
Canagora, Fort, NY   Mohawk River.
Canajohara, Fort, NY   Same as Canagora.
Canal Battery, AL   Mobile.
Canby Battery, AL   Near Mobile.
Canby, Camp, NY   NY City.
Canby, Fort, NM   Mojave River, Navajo County.
Canby, Fort, WA   Cape Disappointment, mouth of Columbia.
Canfield Cantonment, NE   Near Ponca Creek.
Cannatchocari, Fort, NY   Mohawk River.
Canoe Island Reservation, WA   In the Haro Archipelago.
Canyon Chelly, fort at, AZ   Near Chinle.
Canonicut, Fort, RI   Canonicut Isl., Newport harbor.
Cape Disappointment, fort at, WA   Ft. Canby.
Capr Fear, fort at, NC   Ft. Johnston.
Cape Girardeau, armory at, MO
Cape Girardeau, fortifications at, MO
Cape May, fort at, NJ   Ft. Nassau.
Cape Neddick (Neddock), fort at, ME   York County.
Cape Nome, fort at, AK   Ft. Davis.
Cape of Pines, fort on, CA   Harbor of Monterey.
Cape Sable, fort at, FL   Ft. Poinsett.
Capron, Allyn, Camp, KY   At Ft. Thomas.
Capron Battery, SC   At Ft. Moultrie, Sullivans Isl.
Capron, Fort, FL   Opp. Indian River Inlet.
Capsey Battery, NY   At NY City.
Capture, Camp, OH   Hamilton County.
Carey Gratz, Camp, MO   Rolla.
Carillon, Fort, NY   Lake George (see Ticonderoga).
Carleton, Camp, CA   San Bernardino.
Carlin, reservation at, NV
Carlisle Barracks. PA   Carlisle.
Carlisle Battery, KY   Near Covington.

Carlisle, Camp, PA	Near Carlisle.
Carlos Barrancas, Fort, FL	Near Pensacola.
Carlsbad AAF, NM	SW of Carlsbad.
Carlstrom Field, FL	
Carlyle, fort at, IL	
Carmel, Camp, MD	Frederick.
Carneys Bridge, batteries at, LA	Near Pattersonville.
Carolina, Fort, SC	Port Royal.
Caroline, Fort, FL	St. Johns Bluff on St. John's River; became Ft. San Mateo.
Carpenter Battery, ME	At Ft. McKinley.
Carpenter Isl., battery on, DE	Delaware River, nr. Ft. Mifflin.
Carpenter Redoubt, TN	Chattanooga.
Carpenter Redoubt, VA	
Carr, Camp, AR	Big Sugar Creek.
Carrington, Camp, IN	Indianapolis.
Carroll, Camp, MD	Near Baltimore.
Carroll, Fort, DC	1 mi. SE of Giesboro Point.
Carroll, Fort, FL	Pease Creek.
Carroll, Fort, MD	Sollers Point Flats, Patapsco River, 8 mi. below Baltimore.
Carrollton, fortifications at, LA	
Carson, Camp/Fort, CO	5 mi. S of Colorado Springs.
Carswell Field, TX	Ft. Worth.
Carver Gen. Hospital, DC	Washington.
Casa Bianca, Camp, TX	Neuces River.
Cascades, Fort, WA	Near Cascade City.
Casco Bay, fort at, ME	Ft. Loyal.
Casey, Camp, MD	Bladensburg.
Casey, Camp, VA	Alexandria.
Casey, Fort, FL	In Charlotte harbor.
Casey, Fort, WA	Near Port Townsend, Island County.
Casimir, Fort, DE	Delaware River, near Newcastle.
Casino, Fort, TN	Nashville.
Casper AAF, WY	NW of Casper.
Casper, Fort, WY	Platte Bridge.
Cass, Camp, CA	Redbluff.
Cass, Camp, LA	Bay of St. Louis.
Cass, Fort, TN	Cass County.
Cass, Fort, VA	Near Georgetown, DC.
Cassells, fort or castle, PA	Monongahela River, Fayette County.
Cassin, Fort, VT	Mouth of Otter Creek.
Cassville, fort at, WI	
Castine Battery, ME	Penobscot Bay, 9 mi. from Belfast.
Castine, fort at, ME	Ft. Pentagoet.
Castle, The, or Castle William, MA	Boston harbor; later the site of Ft. Independence.
Castle Battery, MS	Vicksburg.
Castle Garden, camp at, NY	NY City.
Castle Isl., fort on, MA	Boston harbor; later site of Ft. Independence.
Castle Isl., fort on, NY	Near Albany; Ft. Nassau.
Castle Pickney, SC	Charleston Harbor.
Castleton, fort at, VT	Ft. Warren.

Castle William, Fort, MA	Boston harbor; later site of Ft. Independence.
Castle Williams, NY	Governors Isl., NY City harbor.
Castlios, Fort, MO	St. Charles County.
Caswell Battery, NC	At Ft. Caswell.
Caswell, Fort, NC	Oak Isl., Cape Fear River.
Cat Isl., reservation, MS	Entrance of Lake Borgne.
Caustens Bluff, fort at, GA	Near Savannah.
Cavallo Point Battery, CA	Cavallo Point.
Cave Hill National Cemetery, KY	Louisville.
Cawakey, Fort, VA	Petersburg.
Cedar, Fort, SD	28 mi. above Pierre.
Cedar Keys, battery at, FL	Gulf of Mexico, SW of Gainesville.
Cedar Keys, reservation at, FL	Cantonment Morgan.
Cedar Point, reservation, AL	Entrance to Mobile Bay.
Cedar Point, battery at, VA	On Lower Potomac.
Cedar Rapids, fort at, IA	
Centre Battery, FL	At Ft. McRee.
Center, Fort, FL	Near Lake Okeechobee.
Central Branch Nat'l. Mil. Home, OH	Montgomery County.
Chadbourne, Fort, TX	Oak Creek, Coke County.
Chadds Ford, fort at, PA	Delaware County.
Chaffee, Camp, AR	
Chain Battery, NY	At Highlands, West Point.
Chain Bridge, battery at, DC	Above Georgetown.
Challam Point, reservation, WA	Entrance to Port Discovery.
Chalmette National Cemetery, LA	Near New Orleans, LA
Chalmette, redoubt at, LA	"
Chambers, Camp, PA	3 mi. from Chambersburg.
Chambers, Fort, IL	Near Lebanon, St, Clair County.
Chambers, Fort, PA	Chambersburg.
Champlain Arsenal, VT	Vergennes.
Chanute Field, IL	Rantoul.
Chapins Bluff, fort at, VA	Near Richmond.
Chaplin, Fort, DC	1 mi. SE of Bennings Bridge.
Chapman Battery, MS	Corinth.
Chapman Field, FL	Near South Miami.
Chapman, Fort, SC	Ashepoo River.
Charity, Fort, VA	Henrico.
Charity Gen. Hospital, LA	New Orleans, LA.
Charlemont, works at, MA	
Charles, Fort, AR	White River.
Charles, Fort, FL	Pensacola.
Charles, Fort, ME	Pemaquid.
Charles, Fort, MO	38 mi. below St Louis, later the site of Rush Tower.
Charles, Fort, MT	Dawson.
Charles, Fort, NY	Kingsbridge.
Charles, Fort, SC	Port Royal.
Charles, Fort, VA	Kicquotan.
Charles, Fort, VA	Richmond.
Charleston AAF, SC	NW of Charleston.
Charleston Arsenal, SC	Charleston.
Charleston Barracks, SC	"

Charlestown Arsenal, MA   Charlestown.
Charlestown, battery at, MA
Charlestown, Fort, NH
Charlestown, works at, MA   The Citadel, French redoubt, Cobble
                                                          Hill Fort, Fort #3, & fort on Winter
                                                          Hill.
Charlotte, Camp, OH   Sippo Creek.
Charlotte, Fort, AL   Mobile; ex-Ft.Conde.
Charlotte, Fort, MN   9 mi. W of Grand Portage Bay.
Charlotte, Fort, SC   Savannah River.
Charlotte Harbor, reservation, FL
Chartres, Fort, IL   Miss. River, near Kaskaskia, in
                                                          Randolph County.
Chase, Camp, MD   On the upper Potomac.
Chase, Camp, OH   Near Columbus.
Chase, Camp, PA   Grays Ferry.
Chatfield Battery, SC   Charleston harbor.
Chatham AAF, GA   NW of Savannah.
Chatham, Camp, TN   Robertson County.
Chattahoochee Arsenal, FL   Chattahoochee.
Chattanooga National Cemetery, TN   Chattanooga.
Chatterton Hill, batteries on, NY   NY City.
Chauncey, Fort, NY   At Sacket Harbor.
Cheat Mtn., fort on, VA
Checaugo (Chicafou), Fort, IL   See Chicago.
Chef Menteur Pass, fort at, LA   Ft. Macomb.
Chehalis, Fort, WA   Grays Harbor, Chehalis County.
Chelan, Fort, WA   Near Lake Chelan.
Cheltons Hills, camp at, PA   Camp William Penn.
Chemung, Camp, NY   Elmira.
Chene, Fort, LA   Near Berwick.
Chenectedi, Fort, NY   See Ft. Clear, Schenectady.
Cheraw Hill, fort at, SC
Cherokee, Fort, SC
Cherrys Fort, SC   Washington County.
Cherry Valley, fort at, VA
Chesapeake & Delaware Canal, fort at, DE Opp. Pea Patch Isl.
Chesapeake Gen. Hospital, VA   Near Ft, Monroe.
Chestnut Hill, Camp, PA   Philadelphia.
Chestnut Hill, post on, PA
Cheteo River, camp on, OR   At mouth of river.
Cheves Battery, SC   Charleston harbor.
Cheyenne Agency, fort at, SD   Ft. Bennett.
Cheyenne Depot, WY   At Ft. D.A. Russell.
Chicago, fort at, IL   Ft. Dearborn.
Chicamauga Nat'l. Park, camp in, GA
Chickasaw Agency, post at, I.T. (OK)
Chickasaw Bayou, batteries at, MS
Chickasaw Bluff, fort at, TN   Memphis.
Chickasaw, Fort, IL
Chickasaw, Fort, MS   Pontotoc.
Chico AAF, CA   N of Chico.
Chikaskia, Camp, OK
Childress AAF, TX   W of Childress.

Childs, Fort, NE	Became Ft. Kearney.
Chillicothe Barracks, OH	Chillicothe.
Chimo, Fort, Canada	Koksoak River, Quebec.
Chinsessing, Fort, PA	Delaware County.
Chinook Point, fort at, WA	Ft. Columbia.
Chipola, Fort, FL	Washington County.
Chissel, Fort, NC	On New River.
Choctaw Point/Bluff, fort at, AL	Ft. Stonewall, near Mobile.
Chokonikla, Fort, FL	On Pease Creek.
Chonaguen, Fort, NY	Became Ft. Oswego.
Chostellux, Fort, RI	Narragansett Bay.
Christanna, Fort, VA	Suth ampton County.
Christina, Fort, DE	Near Wilmington.
Christmas, Fort, VA	Near Lake Harney.
Church Battery, VA	At Ft. Monroe.
Church, Fort, FL	Fernandina.
Churchill, Col., Fort, KY	Cumberland Gap.
Churchill Field, Canada	W shore of Hudson Bay, Manitoba.
Churchill, Fort, NV	Carson River, Churchill County.
Churchman, Camp, GA	Albany.
Citadel, The, MA	Prospect Hill, Charlestown.
City Point National Cemetery, VA	City Point.
Clagett Battery, MD	At Ft. Howard.
Clagget, Fort, MT	
Claiborne, Fort, AL	Alabama Riv., nr. mouth of Limestone Creek.
Claiborne, Fort, LA	Natchitoches.
Claremont Gen. Hospital, VA	Alexandria.
Clark Battery, OR	At Ft. Stevens.
Clark, Camp, AL	Near Mobile.
Clark Field, Philippines	Ex-Camp Stotsenburg, 65 mi NE Manila
Clark, Fort, FL	Ocilla River, Alachua County.
Clark, Fort, IL	Peoria.
Clark, Fort, IN	Opp. Louisville, KY.
Clark, Fort, IA	Became Ft. Dodge.
Clark, Fort, KS	Missouri Riv., nr. Osage City.
Clark, Fort, KY	Louisville.
Clark, Fort, MS	Vicksburg.
Clark, Fort, NC	Hatteras Inlet.
Clark, Fort, ND	Missouri Riv., nr. Mandan.
Clark, Fort, TX	Near Brackettville.
Clark, Fort, VA	Petersburg.
Clarke, Fort, UT	In San Pete Valley.
Clarke's Blockhouse, WV	Marshall County.
Clarksburg, fort at, VA	Harrison County.
Clarks Point, fort at, MA	Ft. Rodman.
Clatsop, Fort, OR	Near mouth of Columbia River.
Claud, Fort, OR	Nashville.
Claverack, Fort, NY	Columbia County.
Clay, Camp, OH	Ohio Riv., 3 mi. E of Cincinnati.
Clay, Fort, KY	Lexington.
Clay, Fort, NE	At Platte Bridge.
Clay Gen. Hospital, KY	Louisville.
Clayton, Fort, Panama	SE side of Panama Canal.

Clear Fork of the Brazos, post of, TX	
Clemison, Fort, MO	Montgomery. County.
Cleveland, Camp, OH	Near Cleveland.
Cliffburn Barracks, DC	Mt Pleasant, Washington.
Clifton, Fort, VA	Appomatox River.
Clifton, Fort, VA	James River.
Clifton Lee, Battery, TN	Knoxville.
Clinch, Fort, FL #1	Amelia Isl., Fernandina.
Clinch, Fort, FL #2	Lake Locha Popka.
Clinch, Fort, FL #3	Withlacoochee River.
Clinch, Fort, FL #4	3 mi. from Pensacola.
Clinton AAF, OH	SE of Clinton.
Clinton, Battery, NY	At Ft. H.G. Wright.
Clinton, Castle, NY	NY City, later called Castle Garden.
Clinton, Fort, NY	West Point.
Cloak, Camp, TN	Near Ft. Henry.
Close, Camp, VA	Near Ft. Lyon.
Closter, Fort, NJ	Bergen County.
Clovis AAF, NM	Clovis.
Clyde, Fort, NY	Freys Bush, 2 mi. SW Ft. Plain.
Coalinga Aux. Field, CA	NW of Coalinga.
Coasters Isl., battery on, RI	
Cobb, Fort, I.T. (OK)	Jct. of Pond Creek & Washita River.
Cobb, Fort, NC	Cobbs Point, nr. Elizabeth City.
Cobble Hill, fortifications on, MA	Charlestown.
Cobble Hill, Fort, NY	Brooklyn.
Cobbleskill, blockhouse at, NY	
Cobbs Hill, Battery, MA	Near Roxbury.
Cobbs Hill, redoubt at, NC	Redoubt Zabriski.
Coburn's Fort, WV	
Cochran, Camp, DC	Washington.
Cochran Field, GA	S of Macon.
Cock Hill, Fort, NY	NY City.
Cockpit Point, battery at, VA	Lower Potomac River.
Cockspur Isl., fort on, GA	Ft. Pulaski.
Cody, Camp, NM	Deming.
Coenties, Battery, NY	NY City.
Coeur d'Alene, Fort, ID	Became Ft. Sherman.
Coffee. Camp, KY	19 mi. S of Richmond.
Coffee, Camp, LA	New Orleans.
Coffee, Fort, I.T., (OK)	At Swallow Rock, Arkansas River.
Coffeyville AAF, KS	NE of Coffeyville.
Colchester, fort at, VT	Ft. Frederick.
Cold Harbor, camp near, VA	Hanover County.
Cold Harbor National Cemetery, VA	"
Cole, Camp, MO	Benton County.
Colerain, Fort, GA	St. Mary's River.
Coles Isl., fortifications on, SC	
Cole's Old Field, camp at, SC	
Colfax Camp, ID	Ada County.
College Hill, Fort, KY	Bowling Green.
Collier, Camp, KY	Lexington.
Collins, Camp, KY	Warsaw.
Collins, Camp, TX	Sherman.

Collins, Fort, CO — Larimer County.
Colorado, Camp, AZ — On Colorado Riv. Indian Reservation.

Colrain, works at, MA
Columbia AAF, SC — SW of Columbia.
Columbia Barracks, WA — Became Vancouver Barracks.
Columbia, fort near, PA

Columbia, Fort, WA — Chinook Point, Pacific County.
Columbia Fur Co., Fort, MN — Traverse Lake.
Columbus AAF, MS — NNW of Columbus.
Columbus Arsenal, OH — Became Columbus Barracks.
Columbus Barracks, OH — Columbus.
Columbus fortifications at, KY
Columbus, Fort, NY — Governors Isl., NY City harbor.
Colville, Fort, WA — In Colville, Valley.
Combes, Fort, MD
Comfort, Fort, NC — Knoxville.
Comfort, Old Point, fort at, MN — Ft. Monroe.
Commercial Point, battery at, MA
Commodore Decatur Aux. Field, GA — W of Bainbridge.
Comstock, Battery, MS — Vicksburg.
Comstock, Fort, TN — Knoxville.
Conakay, Fort, VA — Near Petersburg.
Conanicut, Fort, RI — Newport.
Conanicut Isl., fort on, RI — Ft. Getty.
Conant, Camp, MO — Tavern Creek.
Conant, Fort, MA — Stag Head, Gloucester harbor.
Conception, Camp, TX — San Antonio.
Concho, Fort, TX — Ex-Camp Hatch; jct. of Main & North Conchos.

Concord AAF, CA — NW of Concord.
Concord, Fort, LA — Concordia Parish.
Concordia Camp, TX — Near Ft. Bliss.
Conde, Fort, AL — Near Mobile; became Ft. Charlotte.
Coney, Camp, ME — Augusta.
Confederation, Fort, AL — Jones Bluff, Sumter County.
Confiscation, Fort, TN — Nashville.
Congaree AAF, SC — SE of Columbia.
Connecticut State Soldiers' Home, CT — Noroton.
Connell, Battery, RI — At Ft. Mansfield.
Connelly, Camp, NM — Polvadero.
Conner, Camp, ID — Near Soda Springs.
Connor, Fort, WY — Became Ft. Reno.
Conogohery, fort at, NY — Ft. Rensellaer.
Conrad, Camp, GA — Columbus.
Conrad, Fort, NM — Val Verde, Cocorro County.
Constantine, Fort, AK — Tshugatshian Bay.
Constitution, Fort, NH — Near Portsmouth.
Constitution, Fort, NJ — Became Ft. Lee.
Constitution, Fort, NY — Hudson River, opp. West Point.
Continental Barracks, MA — Boston.
Convalescent, Camp, VA — Near Arlington.
Converse, Redoubt, VA — Sprint Hill on Appomattox River.
Conwell's Fort, PA — Near Merrittstown.
Cony Gen. Hospital, ME — Augusta.

Cook, Camp, CA	NW of Lompoc.
Cooke, Battery, RI	At Ft. Wetherill.
Cooke Camp, MT	Mouth of Judith River.
Coolidge AAF, AZ	S of Coolidge.
Coolidge, Battery, TN	Chattanooga.
Coolidge Field, Brit. West Indies	Antigua
Coombs, Battery, KY	2 mi. W of Covington.
Coon's Fort, WV	In NW part of state.
Cooper, Camp, MO	Howard County.
Cooper, Camp, TX	5 mi. E of mouth of Oteys Creek, Throckmorton County.
Cooper, Fort, FL	Withlacoochee River.
Coos, fort at, NH	
Copper Mine Harbor, fort at, MI	Ft. Wilkins.
Copps Hill, fortifications on, MA	Boston.
Coquille, Fort, LA	Became Ft. Pike (apparently).
Corbin, H.C., Camp, KY	Lexington.
Corbin, H.C., Camp, LA	New Orleans.
Corbin, H.C., Camp, VA	Richmond.
Corcoran, Fort, VA	On Arlington Heights.
Corinth, fort at, VT	
Corinth National Cemetery, MS	Corinth.
Cork Screw, Fort, NY	Long Island; Became Ft. Swift.
Coralers Hook, fort at, NY	
Corn Island, fortifications on, KY	Near Louisville.
Cornwallis, Fort, GA	Augusta.
Coronet Aux. Field, FL	N of Coronet.
Corpus Christi, fort at, TX	Ft. Marcy.
Corvallis AAF, OR	SSW of Corvalis.
Cosmos, Fort, AK	Putnam River.
Cotta, Fort, MT	Missoula County.
Cotton Factory Gen. Hospital, PA	Harrisburg.
Cottonwood. Fort, NE	Cottonwood Springs; became Ft. McPherson.
Cottonwood Springs, fort at, NE	Ft. McPherson.
Couch, Battery, VA	Mouth of Mill Creek.
Couch, Camp, PA	Harrisburg.
Couch, Camp, PA	Philadelphia.
Couty, Fort, NY	Mouth of Niagara River.
Covington, Battery, FL	At Ft. Taylor.
Covington, Fort, KY	Mouth of Licking River.
Covington, Fort, MD	Near Ft. McHenry.
Covington, Fort, NY	Franklin County.
Cow Isl., battery on, ME	Battery Abbott, Lincoln County.
Cowlitz, Fort, OR	Near Cowlitz River.
Cowpens, fort at, MI	
Cox Hill, Redoubt, NY	NY City.
Cox's Fort, PA	Near Gastonville.
Cox's Fort, VA	
Cox's Head, fort at, ME	
Crabbe, Fort, FL	New River.
Craft',s Fort, FL	Near Merrittstown.
Craig, Battery, MA	At Ft. Rodman.
Craig Field, AL	S of Selma.

Craig, Foty, KY	Gilberts Creek.
Craig, Fort, NM	Rio Grande Riv., 3 mi. S of San Marcial.
Craig, Fort, TN	
Craig, Fort, VA	2 m. W of the Long Bridge.
Craig, Fort, LA	Appomattox River.
Crailo (Cralo), Fort, NY	Hudson River, N of Albany.
Crane, Fort, FL	Lake Pithlochoco.
Crane, Fort, FL	7 mi. N of Micanopy.
Craney Isl., fort on, VA	
Cranston, Battery, CA	At the Presidio.
Craven, Battery, AL	Near Nobile.
Craven, Fort, NY	Oneida County.
Crawford, Battery, RI	At Ft. Mansfield.
Crawford, Camp, GA	Chattahoochee River.
Crawford, Camp, TX	Became Ft. McIntosh.
Crawford, Fort, AL	Russell County.
Crawford, Fort, CO	On the Uncompahgre.
Crawford, Fort, FL	Manatee River.
Crawford, Fort, MD	Near Craney Creek.
Crawford, Fort, MI	
Crawford, Fort, PA	Alleghany River, 17 mi. above Pittsburgh.
Crawford, Fort, WI	Miss. River, nr. Prairie du Chien.
Creighton, Fort, TN	Chattanooga.
Cresap's Fort, MD	On N Branch of Potomac River.
Cressel, Fort, CT	On Groton Hts., nr. New London.
Crevecoeur, Fort, FL	St. Josephs Bay.
Crevecoeur, Fort, IL	Lake Peoria.
Crissy Field, CA	Presidio of San Francisco.
Crittenden, Battery, RI	At Ft. Wetherill.
Crittenden, Camp, AZ	Site of old Ft. Buchanan.
Crittenden, Fort, KY	Lexington.
Crittenden, Fort, UT	In Cedar Valley; ex-Camp Floyd.
Crittenden Gen. Hospital, KY	Louisville.
Crocker, Battery, MS	Vicksburg.
Crockett, Fort, TX	Galveston.
Croft, Camp, SC	Spartanburg.
Croghan, Fort, IA	Near Council Bluffs.
Croghan, Fort, TX	On Hamilton Creek, 14 mi above mouth.
Crook, Fort, CA	Fall River, Shasta County.
Crook, Fort, NE	10 mi. S of Omaha, Sarpy County.
Crooked Billet, camp near, PA	Montgomery County.
Crooked Isl. Reservation, FL	St. Andrews Sound.
Crosby, Battery, CA	At the Presidio.
Cross, Battery, MA	At Ft. Rodman.
Cross City AAF, FL	E of Cross City.
Cross, Fort, FL	Palm Point.
Cross, Fort, FL	10 mi. NW of old Ft. Dade.
Cross, Fort, ND	Became Ft. Seward.
Cross, Redoubt, MD	At Ft. Sumner; ex-Ft. Ripley.
Crossman, Camp, PA	Philadelphia.
Crossman, Camp, UT	On Salt Creek.
Crowder, Camp, MO	Neosho.

Crown Hill National Cemetery, IN	Jeffersonville.
Crown Point, battery at, NY	Corlears Hook, NY City.
Crown Point, fort at, NY	Ft. Frederick, Lake Champlain.
Crow's Nest, Battery, VA	Near Dutch Gap.
Crum, Fort, FL	Withlacoochee River.
Crum's Fort, PA	In Stone Valley, Huntingdon County.
Crutchfield, Redoubt, TN	Chattanooga.
Crystal One Field, Canada	Koksoak River, Quebec
Crystal Two Field, Canada	N side of Frobisher Bay, Baffin Isl.
Cuba Libre, Camp, FL	Jacksonville.
Cullum, Battery, FL	Ft. Pickens.
Culpeper National Cemetery, VA	Culpeper.
Cumberland Field, MD	Cumberland.
Cumberland, fort at, MD	Ft. Mount Pleasant.
Cumberland, Fort, VA	
Cumberland Gen. Hospital, TN	Nashville.
Cumberland Head, works at, NY	
Cumberland Isl., works on, GA	St. Andrews Sound.
Cummings, Fort, FL	Withlacoochee River, E of Lumberton.
Cummings, Fort, GA	
Cummings, Fort, NM	At Cooks Mountain Spring.
Cummings, Fort, VA	Petersburg.
Cummings Point, fort/battery at, SC	Ft. Putnam & Battery Gregg; near Charleston.
Cummings, Redoubt, NY	Long Island, near Brooklyn.
Cunningham, Fort, NC	
Cunninghams Isl., fortifications on, PA	In Lake Erie.
Curry's Fort, AL	On the Tombigee River.
Currey, Camp, OR	Silver Creek.
Curtin, Camp, PA	Harrisburg.
Curtin, Camp, PA	Philadelphia.
Curtis, Camp, CA	Humboldt County.
Curtis, Fort, AR	Helena.
Curtiss Field, NY	Mineola.
Cushenoc, Fort, ME	Kennebec River.
Cushing, Battery, MA	At At. Andrews.
Cushing, fort at, ME	Lincoln County.
Cushings Isl., fort on, ME	Ft. Levett.
Custer Battlefield National Cemetery, MT	Crow Agency.
Custer, Camp, MI	Battle Creek.
Custer, Fort, MT	On Big Horn River; ex-Big Horn Barracks.
Custis, Camp, VA	Near Arlington.
Cut Bank Aux. AAF, MT	SW of Cut Bank.
Cuyahoga, Fort, OH	Near Cleveland.
Cuyler Gen. Hospital, PA	Germantown.
Cuyler's Sugarhouse, magazine at, NY	NY City.
Cypress Hills National Cemetery, NY	Brooklyn.

The control tower at Turner Field, Albany, Georgia, during WWII.

Using a BC–221 frequency meter, technicians check out the radio equipment in a WWII trainer.

Dabney, Fort, FL   Suwanee Old Town.
Dade, Fort, FL (original)   Withlacoochee River, 13 mi from Dade's
                                             Battle Ground.
Dade, Fort, FL (later)   Egmont Key, 35 mi. from Tampa.
Dahlgren, Battery, SC   Sullivan's Isl.
Dahlgren, Camp, OR   Crooked River.
Dakota, Fort, SD   Big Sioux River at Sioux Falls.
Dale, Fort, AL   Butler County.
Dale Gen Hospital, MA   Worceater.
Dalghton, Fort, NY   Possibly same as Ft. Dayton.
Dalhart AAF, TX   SW of Dalhart.
Dallas, Fort, FL   Near mouth of Miami River.
Dalles, Fort, OR   Columbia River at The Dalles;
                                             ex-Camp Drum.

Damariscotta, fortifications   at, ME
Danbury, Cantonment, CT   Danbury.
Daniel Field, GA   W of Augusta.
Daniel, Fort, RI
Daniels, Battery, ME   At Ft. Levett.
Daniels, Camp, FL   Near Ft. Myers.
Dannelly AAF, AL   SW of Montgomery.
Dan Russell, Camp, NC   Raleigh.
Danube, Fort, NY   (A stockade fort.)
Danville Branch National Home, IL   Danville.
Danville National Cemetery, KY (2nd)   Danville.
Danville National Cemetery, VA (1st)   Henrico County.
Darby, Fort, LA
Darien, fort at, GA
Darling, Fort, VA   On Drury's Bluff, James River.
Darrell, Fort, SC   Charleston harbor.
D.A. Russell, Fort, WY   Near Cheyenne.
Date Creek, camp at, AZ   60 mi. SW of Prescott; estab. as
                                             Camp McPherson.
Datelan AAF, AZ   W of Aztec.
Dauphin Isl., fort on, AL   Ft. Gaines.
Davant, Camp, TX   Near Baudere Pass.
Davenport, Fort, FL   Reedy Creek, nr. Big Cypress Swamp.
Davids Isl., Depot, etc., NY   Nr. mouth of Little River; became
                                             Camp Beecher.
Davidson, Fort, MO   Pilot Knob.
Davis Blockhouse, PA   Nr. Welsh Run, Center County.
Davis, Camp/AAF, NC   SW of Folkstone.
Davis, Camp, NE   At Platte Bridge, 120 mi. above
                                             Ft. Laramie.
Davis, Camp, VA   Romney, nr. Petersburg.
Davis, Cantonment, IL   Rock River.
Davis, Fort, AL   Macon County.
Davis, Fort, AK   Nome.
Davis, Fort, DC   E of the Eastern Branch.
Davis, Fort, I.T. (OK)
Davis, Fort, TX   Limpia River, Jeff Davis County.
Davis, Fort, VA   Before Petersburg.
Davis, Jefferson, Camp, MS   E Pascagoula.

Davis-Monthan Field, AZ	SE of Tucson.
Davison, Fort, VA	Before Petersburg.
Davis, Redoubt, MD	3 mi. above Georgetown, DC;
	ex-Ft. Alexander.
Day, Camp, MA	Cambridge.
Days Point, battery at, VA	James River.
Dayton, Fort, NY	Mohawk River at Herkimer.
Dead Mans Bay, fort at, FL	Ft. Frank Brooke.
Dead Mans Isl. Reservation, CA	Wilmington harbor.
Dean's Fort, PA	Canoe Valley, Juniata County.
Dearborn Battery, AL	At Ft. Morgan.
Dearborn, Fort, GA	13 mi. SE of Ft. Floyd.
Dearborn, Fort, IL	Chicago.
DeCamp Gen. Hospital, NY	Davids Isl.
Decatur, Battery, MD	At Ft. Washington.
Decatur, Fort, AL	Tallapoosa River.
Deception Pass North Reservation, WA	Two Islands, Island County.
Deception Pass South Reservation, WA	Two Islands, Island County.
Decherd, Camp, TN	Near Decherd.
Decker, Fort, PA	Mouth of Cross Creek, Wash. County.
Deep Creek, fort on, VA	Near Albemarle & Chesapeake Canal.
Deerfield, fortifications at, MA	
Deer Isl., fort on, MA	Boston Harbor.
Defence, Fort, WA	Vancouver Island.
Defiance, Camp, AL	49 mi. W of Chattahoochee.
Defiance, Camp, IL	Jct. of Ohio & Miss. Rivers.
Defiance, Camp, VA	Near New River; probably in Giles Co.
Defiance, Fort, AZ	Canyon Bonita, Apache County.
Defiance, Fort, CA	4 mi. below Ft. Yuma.
Defiance, Fort, FL	
Defiance, Fort, IA	Near Estherville.
Defiance, Fort, MA	Gloucester.
Defiance, Fort, NC	Roanoke Isl.
Defiance, Fort, NY	Red Hook.
Defiance, Fort, NY	Opp. Ticonderoga.
Defiance, Fort, OH	Defiance County.
Defiance, Fort, OR	
Defiance, Fort, TX	Goliad.
Defiance, Fort, VA	Augusta County.
Defiance, Fort, WI	Near Mineralpoint.
Defiance Point Reservation, WA	Narrows of Puget Sound.
De Hart, Battery, ME	At Ft. Williams.
De Hart, Fort, TN	Loudon.
De Kalb, Fort, VA	1 mi. W of Aqueduct Bridge; became
	Ft. Strong.
Delafield, Fort, SC	S end of Folly Isl.
Delancy, Fort, NY	On Bergen Neck.
Delano AAF, CA	S of Delano.
Delaware, blockhouse at, OH	
Delaware, Fort, DE	Pea Patch Isl., near New Castle.
De Leon Battery, FL	At Key West.
De Lesseps, Fort, Panama	Canal Zone
Delphi, fortifications at, NY	
Del Rio, Camp, TX	Near Del Rio, Kinney County.

Del Valle Army Air Base, TX	Austin; became Bergstrom AAF.
Deming AAF, NM	E of Deming.
De Monteil, Battery, NC	On Shallow Bay Bay.
Demopolis AAF, AL	SW of Demopolis.
Denand, Fort, FL	Caloosahatchee River, 20 mi. above Ft. Myers.
Denham, Fort, RI	Narragansett Bay.
Dennison, Camp, OH	Near Miamisville, Hamilton County.
Denonville, Fort, NY	Near Niagara Falls.
Deposit, Fort, AL	Tenn. River, mouth of Honeycomb Creek, Lowndes County.
Deposit, Fort, OH	Near Waterville.
De Ridder AAF, LA	W of De Ridder.
De Russy Battery, VA	At Ft. Monroe.
De Russy, Fort, DC	2 mi. NE of Tennallytown.
De Russy, Fort, HI	
De Russy, Fort, LA	Alexandria.
Des Ecores, Fort, TN	Memphis.
Desert Center AAF, CA	NE of Desert Center.
Deshler's Fort, PA	Near Lehigh River.
Desmares Gen. Hospital, DC	Washington.
Des Moines, Fort, IL	Buffalo Rock.
Des Moines, Fort, IA #1	Mouth of Des Moines River.
Des Moines, Fort, IA #2	Site of present Des Moines.
Des Moines, Fort, IA #3	Near Des Moines.
De Soto, Fort, FL	Mullet Key, 34 mi. from Tampa.
Detroit Arsenal, MI	Detroit.
Detroit Barracks, MI	"
Detroit, Fort, MI	"
Devens, Camp/Fort, MA	Ayer.
Devils Lake, fort at, ND	Fort Totten.
Devin, Camp, WY	Little Missouri River.
Dewey, Camp, MA	South Framingham.
Dewey, George, Camp, SD	Sioux Falls.
De Wolf, Fort, KY	New Shepherdsville.
Dexter Aux. Field #1, MO	SE of Dexter.
Diamond, Fort, NY	Became Ft. Lafayette, NY City.
Dickerson, Fort, TN	Knoxville.
Dickerson, Fort, PA	Wilkes-Barre.
Dickerson, Fort, PA	Wyoming.
Dick Robinson, Camp, KY	Garrard County.
Dickenson, Battery, RI	Ft. Wetherill.
Dickey, Fort, PA	Cumberland County.
Diego, Fort, FL	25 mi. from San Diego.
Digges' Point, fortifications at, VA	
Dillies, Fort, OH	Belmont County.
Dillie's Blockhouse, WV	Opp. Grave Creek.
Dillow's Fort, PA	Hanover Twp., Washington County.
Dilworth, Battery, FL	Ft. Taylor.
Dinsmore's Fort, PA	Washington County.
Dinwiddie, Fort, WV	Jackson River.
Dionysius, Fort, AK	Near mouth of Stikeen River.
Discharge, Camp, CA	Angel Island.
Discharge, Camp, CA	Harrisburg.
Discovery, Fort/Reservation, WA	2 mil. facilities at.

Distribution, Camp, VA	Near Alexandria.
Dix, Battery, NY	At Ft. Wadsworth.
Dix, Fort, MD	
Dix, Fort/Field, NJ	Wrightstown.
Dix, Fort, VA	Near Dt. Powhatan, Suffolk County.
Dixie, Fort, NC	Near New Bern.
Dixon, Fort, IL	
Doane, Fort, FL	Near Big Cypress Swamp.
Dobbs, Fort, NC	20 mi. N of Salisbury.
Dobbs Ferry, fort at, NY	Hudson River.
Doboy Inlet, works at, GA	10 mi. E of Darien.
Dodd, Battery, DE	At Ft. Delaware.
Doddridge's Fort, PA	Buffalo Creek, Washington County.
Dodge, Camp, AR	Little Rock.
Dodge, Camp, IA	Near Des Moines.
Dodge City AAF, KS	NE of Dodge City.
Dodge, Fort, IA	Des Moines River, Webster County; ex-Ft. Clarke.
Dodge, Fort, KS	Ford County.
Dog Island, reservation on, FL	Entrance of St. Georges Sound.
Dog Island Reservation, MS	In Gulf of Mexico.
Dogwood, Camp, VA	Dogwood Gap.
Donaldsonville, Fort, LA	Donaldsonville.
Donelson, Fort, TN	Near Dover, on Cumberland River.
Donelson, Fort, National Cemetery, TN	Dover.
Doniphan, Camp, OK	Near Ft. Sill.
Don't, Fort, LA	Near source of Sabine.
Dorchester, Fort, MA	Near Boston.
Dorchester, Fort, SC	Near Givhans Ferry State Park.
Dorchester Heights, fort on, MA	Ft. Dorchester.
Dothan Field, AL	NW of Dothan.
Double Bluff Reservation, WA	Opp. Fairweather Point.
Doubleday Battery, NY	At Ft. Hamilton.
Douglas AAF, AZ	NNW of Douglas.
Douglas, Camp, IL	Chicago.
Douglas, Camp. WI	Juneau County.
Douglas, Fort, AR	Johnson County.
Douglas, Fort, MA	
Douglas, Fort, UT	3 mi. from Salt Lake City.
Douglas Gen. Hospital, DC	Washington.
Douglass, Battery, PA	Near Lake Erie.
Do-ve-gat, Camp, NY	Coveville.
Dover Arsenal, NJ	Dover.
Dover Field, DE	Dover.
Dover, US Powder Depot at, NJ	Dover; became Dover Arsenal.
Dow Field, ME	W of Bangor.
Downers Station, KS	50 mi. E of Monument.
Downey, Camp, CA	Contra Costa County.
Downing, Fort, FL	Suwanee River, 10 mi. from Micanopy.
Down's Fort, SC	7 mi. below Camden.
Drake, Camp, TN	Near Murfreesboro.
Drake, Fort, VA	Near Richmond.
Drane, Fort, FL	Marion County.
Drawbridge, Fort, VA	Near Suffolk.

Drayton, Fort, SC	Otter Island.
Dreadnought, Fort, SC	Silver Bluff, Savannah River.
Drew, Battery, CA	At Ft. McDowell.
Drum Barracks, CA	Near Wilmington.
Drum, Battery, MA	At Ft. Strong.
Drum, Camp, CA	Near San Pedro.
Drum, Camp, OR	Became Ft. Dallas.
Drum, Camp, TX	Rio Grande, opp. Guerrero.
Drum, Fort, NY	15 mi. NE of Watertown.
Drum, Fort, Philippines	El Fraile Isl.
Drum, Simon, Fort, FL	Near Big Cypress Swamp, Brevard Co.
Drunken Dick Shoals, reservation at, SC	
Drurys (Drewrys) Bluff, fort, VA	James River, near Richmond.
Dry Tortugas, fort at, FL	Ft. Jefferson.
Duane, Battery, NY	At Ft. Wadsworth.
Duane, Fort, SC	Near Beaufort.
Dublin Aux. AAF, CA	NW of Dublin.
Du Boise, Fort, NY	Catskill.
Du Chesne, Fort, UT	Uintah River, Uintah County.
Duck Creek, stockade at, OH	Near Marietta.
Dugway AAF/Proving Ground, UT	NW of Indian Springs.
Dulany, Fort, FL	Puntarassa.
Dummer, Fort, NH	Hillsdale.
Dummer, Fort, VT	Connecticut Riv., nr. Brattleboro.
Dumont, Camp, IN	Near Indianapolis.
Dumont, Camp, KY	Near Shelbyville.
Dumpling Point, fortifications at, RI	Near Jamestown entrance to Narragansett Bay.
Duncan, Battery, CA	At Ft. Baker.
Duncan, Camp, DC	Eastern section of Washington.
Duncan, Fort, TX	Eagle Pass, on Rio Grande.
Dun Glen, Camp, NV	Humboldt County.
Dunnellon AAF, FL	ENE of Dunnellon.
Dunmore, Fort, PA	Site of Ft. Pitt.
Dunnings Creek, fort at, PA	Juniata River.
Du Pont, Camp, DE	Newcastle County.
Dupont, Camp, PA	Near Gettysburg.
Dupont, Camp, WV	Carricks Ford, Tucker County.
Du Pont, Fort, DC	2 mi. SE of Washington.
Du Pont, Fort, DE	Delaware City.
Duportail, Battery, AL	At Ft. Morgan.
Dupres Tower, Fort, LA	Bayou Dupre, Lake Borgne.
Dapui's Fort, PA	Shawnee.
Du Quesne, Fort, FL	
Du Quesne, Fort, PA	Pittsburgh.
Durkee, Fort, PA	Susquehanna Riv., nr. Wilkes-Barre.
Dushane, Fort, VA	Near Petersburg.
Dutchess, Camp, NY	Poughkeepsie.
Dutch Isl., fort on, RI	W entrance to Narragansett Bay; Ft. Greble.
Dutch Point, Cantonment, CT	Near site of Hartford.
Dutton, Battery, NY	At Ft. H. G. Wright.
Dyer, Camp, GA	Augusta.
Dyer, Camp, RI	Bear East Greenwich.
Dyersburg AAF, TN	N of Halls.

A member of the Jackson Artillerists of Philadelphia, sometime around 1850.

Camp Travis, San Antonio, Texas, during WWI.

Eagle Pass AAF, TX	N of Eagle Pass.
Eagle Pass, fort at, TX	Ft. Duncan.
Early, Fort, GA	Flint River, Lee County.
Easley's Fort, AL	Nr. jct. of Alabama & Tombigee Rvrs.
East Bank, fort at, NY	NY City harbor.
East, Fort, NY	Near Oswego.
Eastern Branch National Home, ME	Togus.
Eastern Point, fort at, MA	Gloucester harbor,
East Haven, reservation at, CT	
East Hoosic, fort at, MA	
Eastman, Camp, UT	Chicken Creek.
Eastons Point Battery, ME	At Castine.
Eastport, fortifications, ME	
Eaton, Camp, GA	Cherokee Nation.
Eaton, Camp, MI	Island Lake.
Echore Margot, Fort, TN	Memphis.
Econfinee, Fort, FL	5 mi. above mouth of Econfinee River.
Edgartown, fortifications at, MA	
Edgecomb, Fort, ME	Wiscasset.
Edgewood Field/Arsenal, MD	S of Edgewood.
Edinburg Field, British West Indies	Trinidad
Edisto, Fort, SC	Point of Pines, Edisto Isl.
Edward, Fort, NY	Hudson Riv. at Edward Creek, Washington County.
Edwards, Battery, NJ	At Ft. Mott.
Edwards, Camp, MN	Near Lake Preston.
Edwards, Camp, MA	Pocasset.
Edwards, Fort, IL	Warsaw.
Edwards, Fort, WV	Capon River, Hampshire County.
Egbert, Fort, AK	Eagle City.
Egden, Fort, PA	On branch of Susquehanna River.
Egedesminde Field, Greenland	
Eglin Field, FL	SW of Valparaiso.
Eglin Aux. Fields #1 to #8, FL	Valparaiso area.
Egmont Key, fort at, FL	Ft. Dade.
Eldorado, Camp, AZ	Colorado River, nr. mouth of Eldorado Canyon.
Eldridge Point, fortifications at, MA	New Bedford.
Elfsborg, Fort, DE	Delaware River nr. mouth of Salem Crk.
Eliot Gen Hospital, MO	St. Louis.
Elizabeth, Camp, CA	Alexandria.
Elizabeth Field, NY	Fishers Isl., Long Island Sound.
Elizabeth, Fort, VA	Henrico.
Elizabeth Island, fortifications on, MA	Buzzards Bay.
Elizabethtown, cantonment at, NJ	
Elk River, fort at, AL	Ft. Hawkins.
Elk River, Fort, MD	Mouth of Elk River.
Ellensburg AAF, WA	NE of Ellensburg.
Ellicotts Mills, Camp, KY	10 mi. below Cairo.
Ellington Field, TX	SW of Genoa.

Elliott, Fort, TX	Near head of Sweetwater Creek.
Ellis, Fort, MT	Near Bozeman.
Ellis, Fort, NC	Roanoke Isl., near New Bern.
Ellisburg, fortifications at, NY	
Ellis Isl., fort on, NY	Ft. Gibson.
Ellsworth, Fort, KS	Smoky Hill River, became Ft. Harker.
Ellsworth, Fort, VA	Near Alexandria.
Elmendorf Field, AK	Near Anchorage.
El Paso, fort at, TX	Ft. Bliss.
El Pico, Camp, TX	15 mi. NW of Laredo.
Elsinberg, Fort, NJ	Delaware River.
Elstner, Fort, KY	Louisville.
Embry-Riddle Field, TN	SE of Union City.
Emory, Battery, MD	At Ft. Washington.
Emory Gen. Hospital, DC	Washington.
Emory, Camp, GA	Atlanta.
Emory, Camp, MD	Cumberland.
Emory, Fort, VA	Petersburg.
Emory Upton, Battery, NY	At Ft. Wadsworth.
Engle, Battery, NJ	At Ft. Hancock.
Engle, Fort, KY	Louisville.
English Field, TX	Near Amarillo.
English, Fort, PA	See Ft. Machault.
English Turn, battery at, LA	Near New Orleans.
Enid AAF, OK	SW of Enid.
Envart, Camp, WV	Kanawha.
Ephriam, Fort, UT	Near Salt Lake City.
Ephrata AAF, WA	SE of Ephrata.
Erickson, Fort, VA	Newport News.
Erie, Fort, PA	Erie.
Erwin, Battery, TN	Chattanooga.
Esler AAF, LA	NE of Alexandria.
Esopus, fort at, NY	
Esperanza, Fort, TX	Matagorda Isl.
Espiritu Santo Bay, reservation in, FL	
Essington Aviation Camp, PA	Essington
Estill's Station, KY	Kentucky River, 5 mi. from Richmond.
Estrella AAF, CA	NE of Paso Robles.
Etah Field, Greenland	Kane Basin.
Etches, Fort, AL	Henchenbrook Isl.
Ethan Allen, Fort, VA	Opp. Georgetown, DC
Ethan Allen, Fort, VT	5 mi. from Burlington.
Eustis, Battery, VA	At Ft. Monroe.
Eustis, Fort, VA	
Evans, Fort, VA	Near Leesburg.
Evansport, battery, VA	Quantico Creek.
Everett, Fort, VA	Near Lynnport.
Ewell, Fort, TX	Neuces River.
Exchange, Fort, SC	Charleston.
Exeter, Fort, PA	

Raw recruits march off to get their uniforms at Fort Mead, Maryland, during WWI.

Left: A soldier just prior to WWII proudly shows off his uniform. Right: Several WWI doughboys relax out in front of their tent.

Fairfax National Cemetery, VA	Fairfax.
Fairfield, Fort, CT	Fairfield.
Fairfield, Fort, ME	Aroostook River, Aroostook County.
Fairfield-Suisun AAF, CA	NE of Fairfield.
Fairmont AAF, NE	S of Fairmont.
Falmouth, defenses of, ME	
Falmouth, fortifications at, MA	
Fanning, Fort, FL	10 mi. above mouth of Suwanee River.
Farmers Castle, Fort, OH	Belpre.
Farnsworth, Fort, VA	2 mi. SW of Alexandria.
Farragut, Battery, AL	Near Mobile.
Farry, Battery, ME	At Ft. McKinley.
Far West Barracks, CA	Near Marysville.
Fauntleroy, Fort, NM	Became Ft. Lyon.
Fayette, Fort, NY	Verplanck Point, 3 mi. S of Peekskill.
Fayette, Fort, PA	Pittsburgh, a/k/a Ft. Lafayette.
Fayetteville Arsenal, NC	Fayetteville.
Fayetteville National Cemetery, AR	Fayetteville.
Fearns Battery, TN	Knoxville.
Federal Hill, Fort, MD	Baltimore.
Federal Point, fort at, NC	Ft. Fisher.
Fells Point, battery at, MD	Baltimore.
Fenton, Camp, DC	Washington.
Fenton, Camp, MD	Port Tobacco.
Fenwick, Battery, MD	Ft. Screven.
Fenwicks Isl., fort on, SC	Near Charleston.
Ferguson, Battery, ME	Ft. Levett.
Ferguson, Fort, PA	Carlisle Springs.
Fergusom, Fort, SC	Charleston harbor.
Fernandina, fort at, FL	Ft. Clinch.
Fernandino de Barrancas, Fort, TN	Memphis.
Ferres, Fort, OH	Upper Sandusky.
Ferry Point Reservation, VA	
Fetterman, Battery, CA	At Ft. Rosecrans,
Fetterman, Fort, WY	Nr. mouth of La Prele Creek.
Fetter's Fort, PA	Hollidaysburg.
Fidius, Fort, GA	N bank of Oconee River.
Field, Battery, MA	At Ft. Revere.
Field, Fort, VA	Richmond.
Field Point, battery at, RI	Narragansett Bay.
Fillmore, Camp, AR	Near Ft. Washita.
Fillmore, Fort, NM	Near Mesilla.
Fincastle, Fort, WV	Wheeling.
Findlay, Fort, OH	Findlay.
Finlandt, Fort, PA	Near Philadelphia.
Finley Gen. Hospital, DC	Washington.
Finney. Fort, OH	
Finns Point, fort at, NJ	Ft. Mott.
Finns Point National Cemetery, NJ	Near Salem.
Fireman, Fort, NY	Brooklyn.
Fish, Fort, NY	Harlem area of NY City.
Fish Creek, fort at, NY	Saratoga Springs.
Fisher, Fort, NC	Federal Point, mouth of Cape Fear Riv.
Fisher, Fort, VA	Petersburg.

Fishers Isl., fort on, NY	Ft. H. G. Wright.
Fishing Creek, camp at, SC	
Fishing Creek, Fort, PA	
Fishkill Barracks, NY	Fishkill.
Fitzgerald, Camp, CA	Los Angeles.
Fitzsimons Army Med. Center, CO	Aurora.
Five, Number, Fort, TN	Near Isl. #10.
Five Fathom Hole, fortifications at, GA	Near Savannah.
Flagg Island Reservation, FL	Entrance to St. George's Sound.
Flagler, Battery, NC	Near Ft. Macon.
Flagler, Fort, WA	Marrowstone Point, Puget Sound.
Flag Pond Hill, Battery, NC	Near Wilmington.
Flatbush, redoubt at, NY	Brooklyn.
Flathead, Fort, MT	Clarks Fork branch Columbia River.
Flat Lick, Camp, KY	Knox County.
Fletcher, Fort, KS	Big Creek; became Ft. Hays.
Florence AAF, SC	E of Florence.
Florence National Cemetery, SC	Florence.
Florida Arsenal, FL	Apalachicola.
Florida, Fort, AL	Mobile River.
Florilla, Camp, TX	Medina.
Floud, Camp, UT	Became Ft. Crittenden.
Floyd, Fort, AZ	Mombres River; ex-Camp Webster; later became Ft. McLane.
Floyd, Fort, GA	Okeefinokee Swamp.
Floyd, Fort, NE	Solomons Fork, Republican River, 120 mi. SW of Ft. Kearny.
Fly Slip, breastworks at, NY	NY City.
Fogland Ferry, fort at, RI	Narragansett Bay.
Folly, Fort, CT	A/k/a Ft. Nonsense.
Fontana Barracks, CA	San Francisco.
Foote, Fort, MD	Rosiers Bluff, Potomac River, opp. Alexandria, VA.
Fordham Heights, camp at, NY	Bronx, NY City.
Fornance Battery, SC	At Ft. Fremont.
Fornance, Camp, GA	Macon.
Fornance, Camp, SC	Columbia.
Forrest, Camp, TN	Near Fairfield.
Forrest, Fort, NC	Roanoke Island.
Forse Battery, LA	At Ft. St. Philip.
Forse, Camp, AL	Huntsville.
Forty, Fort, PA	Kingston, Kuzerne County.
Foster Field, TX	W of Telferner.
Foster, Fort, FL	Hillsboro River.
Foster, Fort, FL	In Big Cypress Swamp.
Foster, Fort, ME	Gerrish's Isl., Portsmouth harbor.
Foster, Fort, NC	Roanoke Isl.
Foster Gen. Hospital, NC	New Bern.
Fosters Bank, fort on, FL	In Pensacola Bay.
Foulweather Point Reservation, WA	Entrance to Hoods Canal.
Foundry Gen. Hospital, KY	Louisville.
Four Mile Point, Camp, NY	Near Ticonderoga.
Four, Number, Fort, FL	Cedar Keys.
Four, Number, Fort, TN	Near Isl. #10.

Four, Number, Fort, NH	Near Charleston.
Fowle, Fort, FL	Ocklawha River.
Fox Hill, fort on, RI	Conanicut Isl.; Ft. Getty.
Fox Hill, Fort, MA	
Fox Point, battery, RI	Near Providence.
France Field, Panama	Cristobal, Canal Zone.
Francis E. Warren, Fort, WY	Cheyenne.
Francois, Fort, TX	A/k/a Ft. St. Louis.
Frank Brooke, Fort, FL	Esteinhatchee River.
Frank, Camp, I.T. (OK)	Ardmore.
Frank, Fort, Philippines	Carabao Isl.
Frankford Arsenal, PA	Bridesburg.
Frankford, Camp, PA	Near Frankford Arsenal.
Frankfort, Fort, ME	Kennebec River, 10 mi. below Augusta.
Franklin, Camp, VA	Near Alexandria.
Franklin, Fort, MD	2 mi. above Chain Bridge, near DC; became Redoubt Kirby.
Franklin, Fort, NY	Lloyds Neck, N shore Suffolk County.
Franklin, Fort, OH	Ohio River, near Cincinnati.
Franklin, Fort, PA	Near mouth of French Creek.
Franklin, Fort, PA	Shippensburg.
Fraser Battery, NY	At Ft. Slocum.
Frazer, Fort, FL	Pease Creek.
Frazier's Wharf, fort at, SC	Charleston.
Frederica, Fort, GA	St. Simons Isl.
Frederick AAF, OK	SE of Frederick.
Frederick AAF, TX	W of Hollister.
Frederick, Fort, ME	Near Pemaquid; ex-Ft. George; later site of Ft. William Henry.
Frederick, Fort, MD	Frederick.
Frederick, Fort, MD	Near Hancock.
Frederick, Fort, NY	Albany.
Frederick, Fort, NY	Crown Point.
Frederick (Fraderick), Fort, VT	Lower Falls of Onion River.
Frederick, Fort, VA	New River.
Fredericksburg National Cemetery, VA	Fredericksburg.
Fred Steele, Fort, WY	N fork of Platte River, Caribou Co.
Freeland, Fort, PA	On Warrior's Run, near Watsontown.
Freestone Point, fort at, VA	Lower Potomac.
Freland's Fort, PA	Northumberland County.
Freman's Fort, PA	Washington County.
Fremont, Camp, CA	Palo Alto.
Fremont, Camp, MO	Springfield.
Fremont, Camp, PA	Pittsburgh.
Fremont, Fort, SC	Helena Isl., nr. Beaufort.
French, Fort, NC	Near Wilmington.
French's Creek, fort on, PA	Near Waterford.
French Margrets, Fort, OH	Hocking River, Athens County.
French Redoubt, MA	Ploughed Hill, Charlestown.
French's Creek, Fort, NY	Oswego.
French's Mills Post, NY	Sand River, Franklin County.
Frenchtown, redoubt at, MD	
Friend, Fort, VA	Petersburg.
Friendship, Fort, ME	
Froman's Fort, PA	Chartiers Creek, Washington County.

Fry, Camp, DC   Washington.
Fry, Fort, OH   Near Beverly.
Fry, James B., Camp, ME   Augusta.
Fuller, Fort, WV
Fulton, Fort, FL   Near Big Cypress Swamp.
Funston, Camp, KS   Near Kansas City.
Funston, Fort, VA   Romney.
Furiense Battery, ME   At Castine.
Furman's Fort, WV   S branch of Potomac.
Furnace, Fort, VA   Shenandoah County.

Gadsden, Fort, AL   Near Spanish Fort.
Gadsden, Fort, FL   Apalachicola River.
Gadsden's Wharf, fort at, SC   Charleston.
Gage Aux. AAF, OK   SW of Gage.
Gage, Fort, IL   Randolph County.
Gage, Fort, NY   Lake George.
Gaines, Fort, AL   Dauphin Isl., Mobile Bay, site of old
                                     Ft. Tombigee.
Gaines, Fort, AL   SSE of Eufaula.
Gaines, Fort, DC   Washington.
Gaines, Fort, FL   Gainesville.
Gaines, Fort, GA   Chattahoochee River, Clay County.
Gaines, Fort, MN   Crow Wing Co., became Ft. Ripley.
Gaines, Fort, NY   Plattsburgh.
Gaines, Fort, NY   West Point.
Gaines, Fort, PA   Philadelphia.
Gainesville AAF, TX   NW of Gainesville.
Gale, Fort, FL   Putnam County.
Galpin Battery, TN   Near Knoxville.
Galpin, Fort, MT   Jct. of Milk & Missouri Rivers.
Galpin, Fort, SC   Silver Bluff on Savannah Riv., 12 mi.
                                     below Augusta; a/k/a Ft. Dreadnaught.
Galt, Camp, FL   Near Tampa.
Gamble, Camp, MO   Near St. Louis.
Gamble, Fort, FL   30 mi. SE of Tallahassee.
Gansevoort Battery, NY   At Ft. Schuyler.

Gansevoort, Fort, NY	NY City, foot of 12th & Gansevoort Sts.
Gantt Battery, GA	At Ft. Screven.
Gapron, Fort, FL	Bevard County.
Garden City AAF, KS	SE of Garden City.
Gardenier, Camp, TX	S fork of Neuces River.
Gardiner Battery, FL	At Ft. Taylor.
Gardiners Bay, fort at, NY	Eastern Long Island Sound area.
Gardner Field, CA	NE of Maricopa.
Gardner, Fort, FL	Kissimmee River, nr. Cypress Lake.
Garesche Battery, ME	At Ft. Williams.
Garesche Battery, VA	3 mi. NW of Alexandria.
Garesche, Camp, TN	Murfreesboro.
Gareys Ferry, ordnance depot, FL	Black Creek, Duval County.
Garland Battery, GA	Ft. Screven.
Garland, Fort, CO	Utah Creek, Costilla Co., ex-Ft. Massachusetts.
Garnet Head, battery at, MA	Plymouth.
Garnett, Camp, WV	Near Rich Mountain.
Garrard's Fort, PA	Greene Twp., Greene County.
Garrett, Fort, KY	Woodford County.
Gasper's Fort, TN	
Gasperville Isl. Reservation, FL	Entrance to Charlotte harbor.
Gaston Battery, MA	At Ft. Rodman.
Gaston, Fort, CA	In Hoopa Valley.
Gaston, Fort, NC	New Bern.
Gates, Fort, FL	St. Johns River, 4 mi. S of mouth of Ocklawaha River.
Gates, Fort, TX	Leon River, 5 mi. above Coryells Creek.
Gatewood Battery, VA	At Ft. Monroe, VA.
Gatlin, Fort, FL	Watermelon Lake.
Gavock, Fort, TN	Ft. Donelson, a/k/a Ft. McGavock.
Gay, Fort, WV	Wayne County.
Gayoso, Fort, MO	Gayoso.
Gayoso Gen. Hospital, TN	Memphis.
Geary, Fort, TN	Leesburg, ex-Ft. Johnston.
Geiger Field, WA	SW of Spokane.
George Field, IN	NE of Lawrenceville.
George, Fort, FL	Mouth of St. Johns River, Duval Co.
George, Fort, ME	Castine.
George, Fort, MI	Mackinac Isl.
George, Fort, NY	NY City harbor.
George, Fort, NY	Long Island.
George, Fort, NY	Oswego.
George, Fort, OR	Astoria
George, Fort, PA	
George, Fort, RI	Goat Isl., Narragansett Bay.
George, Fort, VA	Old Point Comfort.
George, Fort, WV	Petersburg.
George G. Meade, Fort, MD	
Georges Battery, ME	Georges River.
George, St., Fort, ME #1	Thomaston.
George, St., Fort, ME #2	Pemaquid.
George, St., Fort, ME #3	Brunswick
Georgetown, fortifications at, ME	

Georgevski, Fort, AK	On Kenyon Bay.
George Wright, Fort, WA	
Georgies Island, fort on, MA	Ft. Warren.
Georgian Gulf Reservation, WA	
German Flats, forts on, NY	Fts. Dayton, Herkimer & Stanwix.
German, camp at, PA	
Gererishs Isl., fort on, ME	Ft. Fisher.
Getty, Camp, VA	Suffolk.
Getty, Fort, RI	Fox Hill on Conanicut Isl.
Gettysburg National Cemetery, PA	Gettysburg.
Gibbon, Fort, AK	Mouth of Tanana River.
Gibbs Field, TX	NW of Ft. Stockton.
Gibbs, Fort, SC	
Gibbs, J.B. Gen. Hospital, KY	Lexington.
Gibson Cantonment, AR	Arkansas River.
Gibson, Fort, I.T. (OK)	Cherokee Nation.
Gibson, Fort, I.T. (OK)	Grand River.
Gibson, Fort, NY	Ellis Isl., NY City harbor.
Gibson, Fort, PA	Hestonville, near Philadelphia.
Gila Bend AAF, AZ	WSW of Gila Bend.
Gila Copper Mines, post at, NM	Ft. McLane.
Gilbert, Fort, MA	Brookfield.
Gill, Camp, KY	Olympia Springs.
Gillem, Fort, TN	Nashville.
Gillespie, Fort, FL	Near Graham, Alachua County.
Gillespie, Fort, TN	Holston River.
Gilliland, Fort, FL	Newnansville.
Gillmore Battery, NY	At Ft. Hamilton.
Gillmore, Fort, VA	At Chapin's Farm.
Gilman, Camp, GA	Americus.
Gilmer, Camp, GA	Okeefinokee Swamp.
Gilmer, Fort, VA	Gloucester Point.
Girardeau, Fort, MO	Capr Girardeau.
Girtys Town, fort at, OH	St. Marys River.
Gladden Redoubt, AL	Near Mobile.
Glade Hollow, Fort, WV	Russell County.
Glasgow Aux. AAF, MT	NE of Glasgow.
Glass Redoubt, AL	Alabama & Tombigee Rivers.
Glen Camp Battery, VA	Near Ft. Corcoran.
Glendale National Cemetery, VA	Glendale, Henrico County.
Glenn, Fort, AK	
Gloninger, Fort, PA	Near Lebanon.
Gloucester, fort at, MA	Ft. Point.
Gloucester Point, fort at, VA	Ft. Keyes.
Glover, Fort, MA	Marblehead harbor.
Glover Battery, SC	James River, near Charleston.
Glower, Fort, OH	
Goat Island, fort on, RI	Ft. Anne, Newport harbor.
Goat Island, fort on, SC	On Stone Inlet.
Goats Point, battery at, GA	Tybee Isl.
Goddard, Camp, PH	Columbus.
Godfrey Battery, CA	At the Presidio.
Godman AAF, KY	At Ft. Knox.
Godolphin, Fort, SC	Same as Ft. Galpin.

Godthaab Field, Greenland	Godthaab.
Goings, Fort, IL	Kaskaskia River.
Golphin, Fort, GA	Augusta.
Goodfellow AAF, TX	SE of San Angelo.
Good Hope, Camp, MD	Near the Eastern Branch.
Good Hope, Fort, CT	Hartford.
Good Hope, Fort, DC	Became Ft. Wagner.
Good Hope, Fort, ME	Near Rolla.
Goodrich, Camp, VA	Middletown, VA
Good Samaritan Gen. Hospital, MO	St. Louis.
Goodwin, Fort, AZ	Gila River, Pima County.
Goose Bay Field, Labrador	Goose Bay.
Goose Island Reservation, WA	In Strait of San Juan de Fuca.
Gordon, Fort, GA	9 mi. SW of Augusta.
Gore Field, MT	SW of Great Falls.
Gorges, Fort, ME	Hog Isl. Ledge, Portland harbor.
Gorham Field, TX	
Gosport, Fort, NH	
Gottenburg, Fort, DE	Tinicum Isl.
Governors Bridge, fort at, SC	Near Charleston.
Governors Island, fort on, MA	Ft. Winthrop.
Governors Island, fortifications on, NY	Castle Williams, Fts. Jay & Columbus.
Gowanus Bay, redoubts at, NY	Brooklyn.
Gowen AAF, ID	SW of Boise.
Gower, Fort. OH	Athens.
Grafton, Fort, VA	4 mi. from Yorktown.
Grafton National Cenetery, WV	Grafton, Taylor County.
Graham Battery, NY	At Ft. Totten.
Graham, Camp, DC	4 mi. N of Washington.
Graham, Camp, GA	Tybee Isl.
Graham, Fort, TX	Brazos River, Hill Co., 14 mi. from Hillsboro.
Graham, Fort, VA	Near Arlington.
Granby, Fort, SC	Near Columbia.
Grand Battery, NY	At Bowling Green, NY City.
Grand Forks Field, ND	W of Grand Forks.
Grand Gulf, fortifications at, MS	
Grand Island AAF, NE	NE of Grand Island.
Grand Island, fort near, NE	Ft. Kearny.
Grand Portage, fort at, MN	Ft. William.
Grand River Agency, camp at, ND	90 mi. above Ft. Sully.
Grand Terre Island, forts on, LA	Fts. Lafitte & Livingston.
Grand Tower Rock, reservation, MO	In Mississippi River.
Granger Battery, NJ	At Ft. Hancock.
Granger, Fort, TN	On Harpeth River.
Granger, Fort, TN	On Holston River.
Granger Gen. Hospital, AL	Huntsville.
Grant Battery, GA	Tybee Isl.
Grant, Camp, IL	Rockford.
Grant, Camp, NY	NY City.
Grant, Camp, VA	Richmond.
Grant, Fort, AZ (first)	Jct. of Arivaypa & San Pedro Rivers.
Grant, Fort, AZ (second)	Foot of Mt. Graham.
Grant, Fort, Panama	Canal Zone.

Grant, Fort, MS	Near Vicksburg.
Grant, Gen. Hospital, OH	Cincinnati.
Grant, Gen. Hospital, NY	Willets Point, NY City.
Grant National Park, camp in, CA	
Grants Island, reservation, AL	In Mobile Bay.
Granville, Fort, NC	Portsmouth.
Granville, Fort, PA	Juniata River, nr. Lewistown.
Gratiot, Fort, MI	St. Clair River, nr. Port Huron.
Gratiot Grove, fort at, WI	
Grattan, Fort, NE	Ash Hollow, Taylor Co., Platte River.
Grave Creek, Fort, WV	Marshall Co.
Gray Field, WA	At Ft. Lewis.
Gray, Fort, NC	Roanoke River, near Plymouth.
Grayling AAF, WI	NW of Grayling.
Great Battery, LA	At New Orleans.
Great Bend AAF, KS	SW of Great Bend.
Great Brewster Isl., reservation, MA	Near Cape Cod.
Great Bridge, fort at, VA	9 mi. from Norfolk.
Great Diamond Island, fort on, ME	Ft. McKinley, Portland harbor.
Great Falls AAF, MT	E of Great Falls.
Great Gull Island, fort on, NY	Ft. Michie.
Great Hog Island, battery on, ME	Portland harbor.
Great Horseshoe Bend, fortified camp, AL	Tallapoosa (Tohopeka) River.
Great Meadow, fort at, NH	Westmoreland.
Great Ossippee Point, fort at, NH	At Great Ossippee Pond.
Great Salt Plains Field, OK	SE of Vining.
Great Warsaw Island, battery on, GA	Near Savannah.
Greble, Camp, PA	Harrisburg.
Greble, Camp, VA	Norfolk.
Greble, Fort, DC	2 mi. S of Giesboro Point.
Greble, Fort, RI	Dutch Isl., Narragansett Bay, near Newport.
Greely, Fort, AK	105 mi. SE of Fairbanks.
Green, Fort, FL	De Soto Co., 30 mi. E of Tampa Bay.
Green, Fort, PA	Site of Rosston, Armstrong County.
Green, Fort, SC	Folly Isl.
Green Bay, fort at, WI	Ft. Howard, & older fort built 1726.
Greenburg, Camp, NY	Tarrytown.
Greenbush, cantonment at, NY	
Greene Battery, RI	At Ft. Adams.
Greene, Fort, GA	St. Marys River.
Greene, Fort, NY	Brooklyn.
Greenfield, works at, MA	
Greenfield, Fort, TN	
Green Hill Road, batteries, RI	
Green Island, batteries on, GA	
Greenleafs Point, defenses at, DC	Became Washington Barracks.
Greenville AAF, SC	S of Greenville.
Greenville, Fort, OH	Miami River.
Greenville, Fort, PA	Western Pennsylvania.
Greenwood AAF, MS	SE of Greenwood.
Greenwood, Fort, MS	Yazoo River, near bend of Tallahatchie.
Greenwood Island, reservation, MS	Pascagoula Bay.
Gregg Battery, NJ	At Ft. Mott.

Gregg Battery, SC	Cummings Point.
Gregg, Fort, VA	Petersburg.
Grenada AAF, MS	N of Grenada.
Grenadier Battery, NY	At NY City.
Grenier AAF, NH	S of Manchester.
Griffin Battery, NY	At Ft. Hamilton.
Griffin, Camp. VA	Lewinsville.
Grierson, Camp, KS	Little Arkansas River.
Grierson, Camp, TN	Memphis.
Grierson, Fort, GA	Augusta.
Griffin, Fort, FL	8 mi. from mouth of Suwanee River.
Griffin, Fort, TX	Clear Fork of Brazos River, Shackelford Co., ex-Camp Wilson.
Griffith Battery, ME	At Castine.
Griswold, Camp, VA	Near Portsmouth.
Griswold, Camp, VA	Near Suffolk.
Griswold, Fort, CT	Groton Heights, New London.
Groton AAF, CT	SE of New London.
Groton Heights, fort at, CT	Became Ft. Griswold.
Grovers Cliff, fort at, MA	Ft. Banks.
Guadelupe River, fort at, TX	Mouth of river.
Guejarros, Fort, CA	Eastern entrance to San Diego Bay.
Guenther, Camp, NY	Exposition Grounds, Buffalo (1901).
Gulf Weather Station Field, TX	E end of Matagorda Isl.
Gulfport AAF, MS	NE of Gulfport.
Gunnison, Fort, UT	San Pete.
Gunters Landing, cantonment at, AL	
Gurnet Point, fort at, MA	Ft. Andrew.
Guyon, Fort, LA	On Bayou La Fourche.
Gwyns Island, camp on, VA	Near Washington, DC

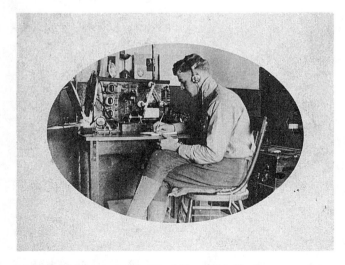

A doughboy at Camp Alfred Vail, in New Jersey, learns how to operate a wireless set during WWI.

Camp Lee, Virginia, as it looked during WWI.

Signal Corps training at Fort Monmouth during WWII.

Haan, Camp, CA	Riverside.
Habersham Battery, GA	At Ft. Screven.
Haddington Gen. Hospital, PA	Philadelphia.
Haddrells Point, reservation, SC	Charleston harbor..
Hagerty, Fort, VA	Near Washington, DC.
Haines Bluff, camp at, MS	14 mi. above Vicksburg.
Hale Battery, RI	At Ft. Greble.
Hale, Fort, CT	E side entrance, New Haven harbor.
Hale, Fort, ND	Missouri River at Lower Brule Agency.
Half Moon Battery, ME	At Castine.
Half Moon Batteries, NC	Wilmington.
Half Moon Fort, MO	St. Louis.
Half Moon, post, NY	14 mi. above Stillwater.
Halifax Field, Canada	Halifax, Nova Scotia.
Halifax, Fort, ME	Kennebec River, above Augusta.
Halifax, Fort, PA	Mouth of Armstrong Creek, Dauphin Co.
Hall, Fort, ID	Snake River, Lincoln Valley.
Hall, Fort, KY	
Hall, Fort, OR	Snake River, nr. Cantonment Loring.
Halleck Battery, GA	At Tybee Isl.
Halleck Battery, NJ	At Ft. Hancock.
Halleck, Fort, KY	Columbus.
Halleck, Fort, NV	Elko Co., 12 mi. S of Halleck Station.
Halleck, Fort, VA	Suffolk.
Halleck, Fort, WY	Foot of Medicine Bow Mountain.
Hallet, Camp, RI	Cranston.
Halletts Point, fort at, NY	Ft. Stevens.
Halliman, Fort, FL	Levy County (probably).
Halt Mont, Fort, NY	
Hamer, Fort, FL	Near mouth of Manatee River.
Hamilton AAF, CA	San Rafael.
Hamilton Battery, GA	On Bird Isl., Savannah River.
Hamilton, Camp, KY	Lexington.
Hamilton, Camp, MD	Buckeyestown.
Hamilton, Camp, TN	Columbia.
Hamilton, Camp, TX	Near Ft. Brown.
Hamilton, Camp, VA	Near Ft. Monroe.
Hamilton, Fort, FL	Madison County.
Hamilton, Fort, NY	Brooklyn side of The Narrows, NY City harbor.
Hamilton, Fort, OH	Hamilton.
Hamilton, Fort, PA	Stroudsburg.
Hamilton, Fort, RI	Rose Isl., Newport harbor.
Hamilton, Fort, UT	
Hamilton, Fort, WI	Lafayette County.
Hammer Field, CA	E of Fresno.
Hammond AAF, LA	NE of Hammond.
Hammond, Fort, GA	Allatoona Pass.
Hammond Gen. Hospital, MD	Point Lookout.
Hammond Gen. Hospital, NC	Beaufort.
Hammond's Fort, ME	Arrowsic Isl., mouth of Kennebec Riv.
Hampden, batteries at, ME	
Hampton Bridge Redoubt, VA	Near Hampton.

Hampton Field, TX	SW of Dallas.
Hampton, Fort, AL	Elk River.
Hampton, Fort, TN	Tennessee River, near Muscle Shoals.
Hampton, Fort, NC	Later site of Ft. Macon.
Hampton National Cemetery, VA	Hampton.
Hancock Barracks, ME	Houlton.
Hancock, Camp, GA	Augusta.
Hancock, Camp, ND	Edwinton.
Hancock, Camp, VA	Brandy Station.
Hancock, Camp, VA	Near Harpers Ferry.
Hancock County Field, MS	SW of Kiln.
Hancock, Fort, TX	53 mi. E of El Paso, ex-Camp Rice.
Hancock, Fort, NJ	Sandy Hook.
Hancock, Fort, WA	Mouth of Columbia River.
Hancocks Bridge, fort at, NJ	Near Salem, Salem County.
Hand, Fort, PA	Kittanning.
Hanging Rock, post of, SC	
Hannas Town, fort at, PA	Westmoreland.
Hanover, fort at, PA	Luzerne County.
Hanover National Cemetery, VA	Hanover.
Hanscom Field, MA	18 mi. NW of Boston.
Hansley Field, TX	
Hanson, Fort, FL	St. Johns River, 13 mi. SW St Augustine.
Harbert's Blockhouse, PA	
Hardee, Camp, MO	At Pitmans Ferry.
Hardees Bluff, fort at, VA	Ft. Huger.
Hardin, Camp, NY	Sand Lake.
Harding AAF, LA	NNE of Baton Rouge.
Hardins Bluff, battery at, VA	On James River.
Hardy, Fort, NY	Hudson River at Schuylerville.
Hareniger, Fort, NY	A/k/a Ft. Herkimer.
Hare's Corner, Camp, DE	Near New Castle.
Harewood Gen. Hospital, DC	Washington.
Harkeman (Harkimer), Fort, NY	A/k/a Ft. Herkimer.
Harker Battery, AL	At Stevenson.
Harker Battery, NJ	At Ft. Mott.
Harker, Fort, KS	Smoky Hill River, ex-Ft. Ellsworth.
Harlan, Camp, DC	7th Street Rd., Washington.
Harlem Heights, fort at, NY	NY City.
Harllee, Fort, FL	Santa Fe River.
Harlingen AAF, TX	NE of Harlingen.
Harmar, Fort, OH	Opp. Marietta.
Harmon Field, Newfoundland	Stephenville.
Harney, Camp, TX	Belleville, on Rio Grande.
Harney, depot, WA	In Colville Valley.
Harney, Fort, OR	Nr. Harney Lake, Grant Co., ex-Camp Steele.
Harper Gen. Hospital, MI	Detroit.
Harpers Ferry Armory, VA	Harpers Ferry.
Harpswell Neck, defenses of, ME	In Casco Bay.
Harrell, Fort, FL	Head of Alcotopa River.
Harriet, Fort, FL	17 mi. NW of St. Marks.
Harriloliz, Fort, FL	Leon County.
Harris Battery, MD	At Ft. Howard.
Harris, Fort, PA	Later site of Harrisburg.

Harris, Fort, TN	7 mi. above Memphis.
Harris Neck AAF, GA	E of South Newport.
Harrison Battery, KY	Near Newport.
Harrison, Camp, OH	6 mi. from Cincinnati.
Harrison, Fort, FL	Clearwater harbor, Tampa Bay.
Harrison, Fort, IN	Near Terre Haute.
Harrison, Fort, MT	4 mi. from Helena.
Harrison, Fort, NY	N of Mohawk Riv., nr. Stone Arabia.
Harrison, Fort, National Cemetery, VA	Varinagrove, Henrico County.
Harrison, Fort, RI	Narragansett Bay.
Harrison, Fort, VA	Chaffins Bluff, James River.
Harrisonburg, fort at, LA	
Harrisons Hill, fort at, PA	Pittsburgh.
Harrod's Fort, KY	Harrodsburg.
Harry J. Jones, Camp, AR	Douglas.
Hartford, Fort, CT	Hartford.
Harts Island Depot, NY	NY City.
Hartsog's Fort, PA	In Woodcock Valley, nr. Marklesburg.
Harsuff, Fort, FL	Pease Creek.
Harsuff, Fort, NE	Loup River, 76 mi. from Grand Island.
Hartshorne Battery, MD	At Ft. Smallwood.
Harvey Brown Battery, NY	At Ft. Hamilton.
Harvey, Camp, WI	Milwaukee.
Harvey Gen. Hospital, WI	Madison.
Harvie, Fort, FL	Caloosahatchee River, later site of Ft. Myers.
Haskell Battery, SC	James River.
Haskell, Camp, GA	Athens.
Haskell, Camp, GA	Macon.
Haskell, Camp, MO	30 mi. from Warsaw.
Haskell, Fort, VA	Near Petersburg.
Haskin Battery, NY	At Ft. Slocum.
Haskin's Fort, OR	Benton County.
Hastings, Camp, PA	Mount Gretna.
Hatbox Field, OK	Muskogee.
Hatch Battery, KY	Near Covington.
Hatch, Camp, TX	Became Ft. Concho.
Hatch's Ranch, post at, NM	65 mi. from Ft. Union.
Hato Field, Netherlands West Indies	Curacao.
Hatteras, Fort, NC	Hatteras Inlet.
Hattiesburg AAF, MS	ESE of Hattiesburg.
Hatton, Camp, TN	Blains Crossroads.
Haven, Camp, CT	Niantic.
Haven, Fort, UT	Carson Valley.
Havenger (Haveniger), Fort, NY	A/k/a Ft. Herkimer.
Havers Island, fortifications on, NY	Mouth of Mohawk River.
Havre de Grace, battery at, MD	
Hawkins, Fort, GA	Ocmulgee River, opp. Macon.
Hawkins Point, fort at, MD	Patapsco River, became Ft. Armistead.
Hawk's Fort, MA	Charlemont.
Hawley, Camp. TX	Galveston.
Hawley, Fort, MT	Missouri River, Dawson County.
Hawn Fort, AL	Tombigee River.
Hawmarket Battery, MA	Boston.
Hawthorne Field, CA	Hawthorne.

Hayes, Fort, OH	Columbus.
Hays, Alex, Fort, VA	Near Petersburg.
Hays Battery, SC	Morris Island.
Hays, Fort, KS	Big Creek, ex-Ft. Fletcher.
Hayward AAF, CA	W of Hayward.
Hayward, Fort, SC	Jct. of Barnwell Creek & Coosaw River.
Hazelhurst Field, NY	Mineola.
Hazlett, Fort, VA	Near Norfolk.
Hazzard Battery, NY	At Ft. Schuyler.
Head, Fort, MA	Later site of Ft. Sewell.
Head's Fort, MO	N of Rocheport.
Heart Battery, MD	At Ft. Carroll.
Heath, Camp, NC	Morganton.
Heath, Fort, MA	Near Winthrop.
Hedges, Fort, WV	Martinsburg.
Heileman, Fort, FL	Jct. of N & S forks of Black Creek.
Heiman, Fort, KY	Tennessee River, 75 mi. from Paducah.
Helen, Fort, AK	Tshugatshian Bay.
Helena Redoubt, AR	Helena.
Hell, Fort, VA	Petersburg, actually Ft. Sedgwick.
Hell Gate, defenses at, NY	NY City, waters NE of Manhattan.
Helsinburg, Fort, NJ	Same as Elsinburg.
Hembree, Fort, NC	Cherokee County.
Hempstead, camp at, NY	Nassau County, Long Island; Camp Black.
Hempstead, Fort, MO	Howard County.
Hempstead Plains Field, NY	Mineola, Long Island.
Hendershott, Camp, IA	Davenport.
Henderson, Fort, AL	Lee County.
Henderson, Fort, GA	St. Marys River, near Colerain.
Henderson, Fort, LA	New Orleans.
Hendrel, Fort, NC	
Hendrick, Fort, NY	Mohawk River, 30 mi. below Herkimer.
Hendricks, Fort, PA	Snyder County.
Henlopen, Cape, fort at, DE	
Henrico, stockade at, VA	
Henrietta, Fort, OR	
Henrietta, Fort, WA	In Willamette Valley.
Henry, Fort, FL	In the Everglades.
Henry, Fort, ID	Henry Branch of Snake River.
Henry, Fort, MO	Randolph County.
Henry, Fort, NY	Lake George.
Henry, Fort, PA	Schuylkill County.
Henry, Fort, TN	Stewart Co. between Cumberland & Tennessee Rivers.
Henry, Fort, TN	S branch of Holston River.
Henry, Fort, VA	Petersburg.
Henry, Fort, VA	Southampton River.
Henry, Fort, WV	Wheeling.
Henry, Patrick, Camp, MS	Jackson.
Henshaw's Fort, PA	
Hensley Field, TX	SW of Dallas.
Henting Battery, DE	At Ft. Delaware.
Herbert, Hilary A., Camp, AL	Montgomery.
Hereford AAF, AZ	W of Hereford.
Herington AAF, KS	E of Herington.

Herkimer, Fort, NY	Mohawk River at Herkimer.
Hero, Camp/Fort, NY	Montauk Point, Suffolk County.
Heron Island, fort on, AL	Ft. Powell.
Herriam, Fort, UT	At Salt Lake.
Herron, Camp, MO	Pilot Knob,
Herrons Hill, fort at, PA	Pittsburgh.
Hestonville Camp, PA	Philadelphia.
Het huys de Hoop, Fort, CT	Hartford.
H. G. Wright, Fort, NY	Fishers Isl., NE of Long Island.
Hiawasee, Fort, TN	Tennessee River, a/k/a Hiwassee.
Hickam Field, HI	9 mi. W of Honolulu.
Hickenlooper Battery, MS	Vicksburg.
Hickman, fortifications at, KY	Near KY/TN state line.
Hicks, Camp, MD	Near Frederick.
Hicks Gen. Hospital, MD	Baltimore.
Hicksford Barracks, VA	Richmond.
Higgins's Blockhouse, KY	Near Cynthiana.
Highlands, fortifications at, NY	Hudson River.
Highwassee, Fort, TN	Tennessee River, a/k/a Hiwasee.
Higley, Fort, TN	Knoxville.
Hill Battery, MS	At Vicksburg.
Hill, Camp, VA	Near Harpers Ferry.
Hill Field, UT	S of Ogden.
Hill, Fort, CA	Monterey.
Hill, Fort, CT	Near Groton Heights.
Hill, Fort, IL	Lake Co., E side of Shoal Creek.
Hill, Fort. KY	Louisville.
Hill, Fort, ME	
Hill, Fort, MD	Cumberland.
Hill, Fort, MA	Boston.
Hill, Fort, NJ	
Hill, Fort, NY	Auburn.
Hill, Fort, NY	Buffalo.
Hill, Fort, NY	Elmira.
Hill, Fort, NY	Genesee County.
Hill, Fort, OH	Butler County.
Hill, Fort, OH	Highland County.
Hill, Fort, SC	On estate of John C. Calhoun, Pickens County.
Hill, Fort, TN	Knoxville.
Hill, Fort, VA	Petersburg.
Hillsboro Aux. Field, OR	NE of Hillsboro.
Hillsboro, camp at, NC	Orange County.
Hillsborough AAF, FL	N of Tampa.
Hillsgrove AAF, RI	Providence.
Hills Point, battery at, NC	Near Washington, Beaufort Co.
Hills Point, fort at, MD	Annapolis.
Hills Point, redoubt at, VA	Near Suffolk.
Hindman, Fort, AR	At Arkansas Post.
Hindman, Fort, TN	Chattanooga.
Hinds County Aux. Field #2, MS	N of Bolton.
Hinsdale, Fort, NH	Hinsdale.
Hiwasee, Fort, TN	Nr. jct. of Hiwasee & Tennessee Rivers.
Hoarkill, Fort, DE	Lewes, on Delaware Bay.

Hobart Battery, ME	At Ft. Williams.
Hobbs AAF, NM	NW of Hobbs.
Hobbs AAF Aux. #2, NM	E of Lovington.
Hobkirks Hill, redoubt at, SC	Near Camden.
Hobson, Camp, GA	Lithia Springs.
Hobson, Camp, KY	Taylor County.
Hobson, Fort, KY	Near Glasgow.
Hobson's Choice, Camp, OH	Near Cincinnati.
Hoffman, Camp, KS	Near Ft, Leavenworth.
Hoffman, Camp, MD	Baltimore.
Hoffman, Camp, MD	Point Lookout.
Hog Island Ledge, fort on, ME	Ft. Gorges.
Hokessen, Camp, DE	New Castle County.
Holbrook Battery, SC	On Morris Isl.
Holliday's Fort, PA	Near Hollidaysburg.
Holly, Camp, VA	Near Newmarket.
Holly, Fort, VA	On the Darbytown road.
Holmarks Station, fort at, TN	On Bull Run.
Holmes Battery, NC	Smiths Isl., mouth of Cape Fear River.
Holmes, Camp, TX	On Rio Grande, 10 mi. above Ft. Bliss.
Holmes, Fort, FL	11 mi. from Palatka,
Holmes, Fort, I.T. (OK)	Choteau, on the Canadian River.
Holmes, Fort, MI	Mackinac Isl.
Holmes Hole, fortificatons at, MA	Near Vineyard Haven.
Holston Gen. Hospital, TN	Knoxville.
Holt Battery, KY	Near Newport.
Holt, Fort, KY	Ohio River, opp. Cairo, IL
Holt, Joe, Camp, IN	Jeffersonville.
Holt, Joe, Camp, KY	Louisville.
Homestead AAF, FL	WNW of Homestead.
Homestead Field, HI	
Hondo AAF, TX	NW of Hondo.
Honeycutt Battery, ME	At Ft. McKinley, Great Diamond Isl.
Honey Hill, battery at, SC	3 mi. from Grahamville.
Honymans Hill, battery on, RI	
Hood, Fort, TX	N of Killeen.
Hoods Head, reservation at, WA	Admiralty Inlet.
Hoods Point, battery at, VA	On lower Potomac.
Hook, Fort, FL	20 mi. from Ft. King.
Hooker, Camp, MD	Charles County.
Hooker, Camp, MD	Frederick Junction.
Hooker, Camp, VA	Near Ft. Lyon.
Hooker, Joe, Camp, VA	Drummondstown.
Hooper Battery, KY	Near Covington.
Hoosic, Fort, MA	A/k/a Ft. Massachusetts.
Hoover, Fort, VA	Rockingham County.
Hope AAF, AR	NW of Hope.
Hope, Fort, CT	See Good Hope.
Hope, Fort, NY	
Hopeless Chase, KY	Pikesville.
Horn, Fort, MD	Severn River, opp. Annapolis.
Horn, Fort, NY	Near Bloomingdale.
Horn's Fort, PA	3 mi. above Crispins Run, Lycoming Co.

Horn Hook, battery at, NY	NY City, Thompson Battery.
Horn Island Reservation, MS	
Horseshoe Bend, fortifications at, AL	Tallapoosa River.
Horton, Fort, KY	Near Louisville.
Hoskins, Camp, KY	Near Somerset, Pulaski County.
Hoskins, Fort, OR (2nd)	Siletz River, 40 mi. W of Corvallis.
Hoskins, Old Fort, OR (1st)	Willamette River, 6 mi. N of Corvallis.
Hospital Point, battery, at VA	Portsmouth.
Hot Springs Reservation, AR	Garland County, Army/Navy hospital.
Houghtaling, Camp, IL	Mississippi River, near Cairo.
Houlton AAF, ME	Houlton.
Houlton, barracks at, ME	Hancock Barracks.
House Island, fort on, ME	Ft. Scammel, Portland harbor.
House of Good Hope, Fort, CT	See Good Hope.
Houston, Fort, TN	Nashville.
Houston, Sam, Fort, TX	San Antonio.
Hovey, Fort, MO	Ironton.
Howard, Camp, VA	Alexandria.
Howard, Camp, ID	Three Mile Creek, 2 mi. from Mt. Idaho.
Howard Field, Panama	SW bank of Panama Canal, Canal Zone.
Howard, Fort, MD	North Point, Patapsco River, 11 mi. below Baltimore.
Howard, Fort, MI	Fox River, nr. Lake Michigan.
Howard, Fort, MO	40 mi. above St. Louis.
Howard, Fort, WI	Green Bay.
Howard, Fort, VA	Near Petersburg.
Howard, O.O., Camp, WY	Pine Bluffs.
Howe Battery, CA	At the Presidio.
Howe, Camp, NY	Scarsdale, Westchester, County.
Howe, Fort, NY	Lake Champlain, near Ticonderoga.
Howe, Fort, PA	Pittsburgh.
Howell, Fort, SC	Hilton Head.
Howell's Fort, MO	Lincoln County.
Howell's Fort, MO	St. Charles County.
Howlands Ferry, fort at, RI	Newport harbor.
Howlett Battery, VA	Dutch Gap.
Hoy's Fort, KY	Elkhorn River.
Huachuca, Fort, AZ	Mouth of Central Canyon, Huachuca Mountains, Cochise County.
Huachuca, Fort, Aux. AAF, AZ	At Ft. Huachuca.
Hualpai, Camp, AZ	Mojave Creek, ex-Camp Toll Gate.
Hubbardton, Camp, VT	Castleton.
Hubert Street Battery, NY	NY City, North Battery.
Huddleston, Camp, VA	Big Falls Creek.
Hudson Battery, NY	At Ft. Wadsworth.
Hudson, Camp, TX	Devils River, 80 mi. from Ft. Clark.
Hudson, Fort, FL	Near St. Augustine.
Huff, Fort, PA	Mouth of Lycoming Creek.
Huger, Fort, AL	Near mouth of Tensas River.
Huger, Fort, NC	Roanoke Isl.
Huger, Fort, SC	Near Charleston.
Huger, Fort, VA	Hardees Bluff, James River.
Hughes, Fort, GA	Bainbridge, Decatur County.
Huguenin's Plantation, battery at, SC	

Hulbert, Fort, FL	Taylor County.
Hulen, Camp, TX	Near Port Lavaca.
Hull, Fort, AL	5 mi S of Tuskegee.
Hull, Fort, GA	Chattahoochee River.
Humboldt, barracks at, TN	Swayne Barracks.
Humboldt, Fort, CA	Bucksport, Humboldt Bay.
Humphreys Battery, MD	At Ft. Washington.
Hunnewell's Point, fort at, ME	Fort Popham.
Hunt Barracks, NY	NY City.
Hunt, Fort, VA	Potomac River, opp. Ft. Washington, MD.
Hunter, Camp, MO	Scott County.
Hunter, Field, GA	SW of Savannah.
Hunter, Fort, FL	St. Johns River, near Palatka.
Hunter, Fort, NY	Mohawk River, mouth of Schoharie Creek, Montgomery County.
Hunter, Fort, PA	Fishing Creek, Dauphin County.
Hunter, Fort, TN	Cumberland Gap.
Hunter-Liggett, Fort, CA	Monterey Peninsula.
Huntington Smith, Fort, TN	Near Knoxville.
Huntstown, post at, MA	Site of Ashfield.
Hurricane Island Reservation, FL	In St. Andrews Bay.
Hutchinson, Fort, KY	Near Mt. Sterling.
Hyannis Field, MA	N of Hyannis.
Hyde, Fort, NC	At Old Topsail Inlet.
Hyndshaw, Fort, PA	12 mi. from Stroudsburg.

The mortar ranging control room at Fort H.G. Wright during WWI.
This fort, which was located on Fishers Island, east of Long Island
Sound, was deactivated long ago. Its gun emplacements still exist.

Iaqua, Camp, CA	Humboldt County.
Iberville, fort, KY	Mississippi River.
Ibura Field, Brazil	Recife.
Ignatius, Fort, MI	Mackinac Island.
Ilges, Camp, AZ	On Rio Verde.
Ikateq Field, Greenland.	
Illinois, Fort, IL	
Independence AAF, KS	SE of Bolton.
Independence, Fort, CA	Oak Creek, in Owens River Valley.
Independence, Fort, MA	Castle Island, Boston harbor.
Independence, Fort, NY	Hudson River, near Peekskill.
Independence, Fort, NY	On Tetards Hill, between Kingsbridge & Yonkers.
Independence, Fort, VT	Opp. Ticonderoga.
Independent Battery, NY	At NY City.
Indiana State Soldier's Home, IN	Lafayette.
Indianapolis Arsenal, IN	Indianapolis.
Indian, Fort, MT	Missouri River, opp. mouth of the Porcupine.
Indian, Fort, NY	
Indian, Fort, RI	Kingston.
Indian, Fort, MD	
Indian Head, battery at, MD	25 mi. below Washington, on Potomac.
Indian Springs Field, NV	NW of Las Vegas.
Indiantowngap, Fort, PA	3 mi. E of Harrisburg.
Industry, Fort, OH	Toledo.
Infantry Camp, AZ	Became Camp Pinal.
Ingalls Battery, ME	At Ft. McKinley.
Inge, Fort, TX	Leone River, Uvalde County.
Ingersoll, Fort, AL	
Ingersoll, Fort, GA	
Ingolgsby, Fort, NY	Hudson River, Saratoga County.
Iowa State Soldiers' Home, IA	Marshalltown.
Ipitanga Field, Brazil	Bahia.
Ira Harris Battery, VA	Warwick River.
Ira Harris Gen. Hospital, NY	Albany.
Iredell, Fort, NC	Iredell County.
Irish's Redoubt, RI	
Iron Banks, batteries at, KY	Mississippi River, 3 mi. above Columbus.
Irondequoit, Fort, NY	Lake Ontario, at mouth of Irondequoit Bay.
Irons, Battery, MD	At Ft. Armistead.
Ironsides, Camp, NY	Staten Island.
Iroquois, Fort, NY	
Irwin Battery, VA	At Ft. Monroe.
Irwin, Fort, CA	Riverside.
Isabel, Point, fort at, TX	Ft. Polk.
Island, Fort, RI	In Newport harbor.
Island No. 10, batteries on, KY	Mississippi River.
Island Point, fort at, NY	Lake Champlain.
Islington Gen. Hospital, PA	Philadelphia.
Ives, Camp, TX	4 mi. from Camp Verde.
Izard, Fort, FL	Withlacoochee River.

A member of the First Company of Montgomery Guards,
51st Regiment, New York State Infantry, about 1850.

In 1933, a replica of Fort Dearborn was built. It was later dismantled.

Jack, Fort, NC	Near Wilmington.
Jack Adams Battery, MA	At Ft. Warren.
Jackson Barracks, LA	Near New Orleans, ex New Orleans Barracks.
Jackson, Camp, LA	New Orleans.
Jackson, Camp, MO	Near St. Louis.
Jackson, Camp, OH	Goodale Park, Columbus.
Jackson, Camp, TX	Rodeo, 20 mi. from Eagle Pass.
Jackson, Fort, AL	Jct. of Coosa & Tallapoosa Rivers; site of former Ft. Tholouse.
Jackson, Fort, FL	13 mi. SW of Tallahassee.
Jackson, Fort, GA	Became Ft. Oglethorpe.
Jackson, Fort, LA	Mississippi River, 65 mi. below New Orleans, opp. Ft. Phillip.
Jackson, Fort, NY	St Lawrence County.
Jackson, Fort, SC	6 mi. E of Columbia.
Jackson, Fort, WI	Mineral Point.
Jackson, Fort, VA	S end of Long Bridge, opp. Wash. DC.
Jackson, Fort, VA	Manassas Junction.
Jackson, Fort, VA	Richmond.
Jackson Gen Hospital, TN	Memphis.
Jacks Point, fort at, MA	Ft. Sewell.
James, Fort, SD	James River jct. with Shell Creek.
James, Fort, GA #1	Altamaha River, 2 mi. above mouth of Beards Creek.
James, Fort, GA #2	Ogeechee River.
James, Fort, NY	NY City.
James, Fort, VA	Chickahominy River.
James, Fort, VA	Jamestown.
James Island, cantonment on, SC	
Jameson Battery, DC	Eastern branch of Potomac.
Jameson, Camp, VA	Near Ft. Lyon.
Jameson, Fort, SC	
Jamestown, forts near, VA	Fts. James & Powhatan.
Jaqua, Camp, CA	NW California, see Iaqua.
Jarretts Fort, PA	Whitley Creek, Greene, Co.

Jarvis Gen. Hospital, MD	Baltimore.
Jasper Battery, SC	At Ft. Moultrie, Sullivans Isl.
Jay, Fort, NY	Governors Isl., NY City harbor.
Jefferson Barracks, MO	10 mi. below St. Louis.
Jefferson Barracks, NY	
Jefferson Barracks National Cemetery, MO	At Jefferson Barracks.
Jefferson City National Cemetery, MO	Jefferson City.
Jefferson, Fort, FL	At Dry Tortougas.
Jefferson, Fort, KY	Mississippi River, 5 mi. below Cairo, IL.
Jefferson, Fort, NY	
Jefferson, Fort, OH	Darke Co., 5 mi. S of Greenville.
Jefferson Street Battery, TN	Memphis.
Jeffersonville Quartermaster Depot, IN	Jeffersonville.
Jeffreys Hook, battery at, NY	
Jekyl Island, battery on, GA	Near Savannah.
Jenkins, Fort, PA	Susquehanna River, 8 mi. above Wilkes-Barre.
Jenkins, Fort, PA	Westmoreland County.
Jennings, Fort, FL	Wakasassa River, 12 mi. above mouth.
Jennings, Fort, OH	Auglaize River, Putnam County.
Jennison, Camp, MO	Kansas City.
Jericho, Fort, VA	Near Suffolk.
Jerrys Point, fort at, NH	Ft. Stark, Portsmouth harbor.
Jersey Battery, NY	NY City, between Reade & Duane Sts.
Jersey, Camp, DC	On Meridian Hill, Washington.
Jersey City Point, battery at, NJ	
Jersey, Fort, NY	Port Jervis.
Jesup Battery, SC	At Ft. Fremont.
Jesup, Fort, LA	25 mi. SW of Natchitoches, Sabine Co.
Joe Holt, Camp, IN	Jeffersonville.
Joe Holt, Camp, KY	Near Louisville.
John, Fort	American Fur Company's Fort.
John Hay, Camp, Philippines	Baguio Mtn., Luzon.
Johnson, Andy, Camp, TN	Nashville.
Johnson, Camp. PA	Lancaster.
Johnson, Fort, NY	Mohawk River, 3 mi. W of Amsterdam.
Johnson, Fort, SC	James Isl., Charleston harbor.
Johnson's Island, fort on, OH	Near Sandusky.
Johnston, Camp, AL	Mobile.
Johnston, Camp, VA	Near Ft. Lyon.
Johnston, Fort, IL	Warsaw.
Johnston, Fort, NC	Near Southport.
Johnston, Fort, UT	In Cedar Valley.
Johnston, Fort, VA	Leesburg, became Ft. Geary.
Johnston, Fort, VA	Near Richmond.
Johnstown, Fort, NY	Schoharie County.
Jones, Fort, AL	Near Roanoke, Randolph County.
Jones, Fort, CA	In Scotts Valley, Siskiyou County.
Jones, Fort, FL	Aucilla River.
Jones, Fort, KY	Near Colesburg.
Jones, Fort, OR	Willamette Valley.
Jones, Fort, TN	Johnsonville.
Jones, Harry J., Camp, AR	Douglas.
Jones Hill, battery at, NY	NY City.

Jones Island, fort on, GA	Ft. Vulcan, Savannah River.
Jones Redoubt, TN	Chattanooga.
Jordan's Fort, IL	
Jordan, Camp, NC	Roanoke Isl.
Jordan Cantonment, WA	In valley of San Francisco Borgia.
Josephine, Fort, FL	
Joseph T. Robinson, Camp, AR	Conway, ex-Camp Pike.
Josiah Simnpson Gen. Hospital, VA	At Ft. Monroe.
Journey's Fort, IL	Ariston.
Juan de Fuca, Straits of, reservation, WA	
Judiciary Square Gen Hospital, DC	Washington.
Junandat, Fort, OH	Sandusky River.
Jupiter, Fort, FL	3 mi. from Jupiter Inlet.

A soldier during the Spanish–American War poses with his .45–70 rifle.

In WWII, War Bonds purchased by the people of Piqua, Ohio, paid for this Air Corps B–24 Liberator, dubbed the "Piqua Bondolear." Here it is being turned over to the Air Corps at Wright–Patterson AAF by some local Piqua residents, one of whom holds a plaque.

Signal Corps training at Fort Monmouth during WWII.

Kahokia, Fort, IL	
Kalorama Gen. Hospital, DC	Washington.
Kamehameha, Fort/Mil. Reservation, HI	NW of Honolulu.
Kanawha, Camp, WV	Point Pleasant.
Kansas State Soldiers' Hone, KS	Fort Dodge, KS.
Kapala Field, HI	
Karnasch, Fort, KY	Near Louisville.
Kasimir, Fort, DE	Delaware River, at New Castle; a/k/a Ft. Trinity.
Kas Kanong, Fort, WI	Lake Kas Kanong.
Kaskaskia, Fort, IL	Kaskaskia.
Kasonda, Fort, NY	Same as Ft. Onondaga.
Kaye Field, MS	9 mi. N of Columbus.
Keais, Fort, FL	Near Big Cypress Swamp.
Kearny AAF, NE	NE of Kearny.
Kearny Battery, ME	At Ft. Preble.
Kearny Battery, SC	Near Charleston.
Kearny, Camp/Field, CA	N of San Diego.
Kearny, Camp, LA	Carrollton.
Kearny, Camp, VA	Near Alexandria Seminary.
Kearny, Camp, IA	Near Davenport.
Kearny, Fort, DC	Near Tennallytown.
Kearny, Fort, NE (first)	Missouri River, 50 mi. S of Omaha.
Kearny, Fort, NE (second)	On Grand Isl., Platte River.
Kearny, Phil, Fort, KY	Near Newport.
Kearny, Phil, Fort, WY	Big Horn Mtns, between Big & Little Piney forks of Powder River.
Keene, Fort, NY	
Keene, Fort, VA	
Keer's Fort, GA	
Keesler Field, MS	W of Biloxi.
Keifer, Camp, NY	Troy.
Keller's Fort, WV	
Kelley, Fort, VA	On New Creek.
Kellog's Grove, fort near, IL	
Kelly Battery, NY	At Ft. Terry.
Kelly Field, TX	SW of San Antonio.
Kemble Battery, DC	Near Chain Bridge.
Kenay, Fort, AK	Site of old Ft. St. Nicholas, Cook's Inlet.
Kendrick Battery, ME	On Cushing Island, at Ft. Levett.
Kenesaw Mount, fortifications at, GA	
Kenly, Camp, MD	Near Williamsport.
Kennebec Arsenal, ME	Augusta.
Kennebec River, fortifications at, ME	Mouth of river.
Kennedy's Fort, MO	Wright City.
Kennicott, Fort, AK	Near Ft. Nulato.
Kent, Camp, UT	At Ft. Douglas.
Kent, Fort, ME	Jct. of Fish & St. Johns Rivers, Aroostook County.
Kent, Fort, MD	Kent Isl.
Kenton, Camp, KY	Near Maysville.
Kenton's Station, KY	Near Washington.

Kentucky, Fort, NY	Near Sacket Harbor.
Keogh, Fort, MT	Near mouth of Tongue River, Custer Co.
Keokuk National Cemetery, IA	Keokuk.
Kettle Point, battery at, RI	Narragansett Bay.
Key Battery, MD	At Ft. Howard.
Keyes, Camp, ME	Near Augusta.
Keyes, Camp, VA	Near Romney.
Keyes, Camp, VA	On Uptons Hill.
Keyes, Fort, FL	
Keyes, Fort, VA	At Gloucester Point.
Keyser, Fort, NY	Montgomery County.
Keystone AAF, FL	SW of Camp Blanding.
Keystone, Camp, DC	Near Tennallytown.
Key West Barracks, FL	Key West.
Key West, fort at, FL	Ft. Taylor.
Kiawah Island, fortifications on, SC	
Kienuka, Fort, NY	Near Lewiston; Indian fort.
Kilauea Military Camp, HI	Oahu.
Kilmer, Camp, NJ	
Kincade's Fort, MO	Howard County.
Kinckston's Stockade, KY	
Kinderhook, forts at, NY	
Kindley Field, Bermuda	Hamilton.
Kindley Field, Philippines	Corregidor Isl.
King Battery, NY	At Ft. Totten.
King, Camp, KY	Near Covington.
King, Camp, VA	Alexandria.
King, Fort, FL	Ocklawha River.
King, Fort, NY	
King, Fort, TN	Near Chattanooga.
King George, Fort, GA	
Kingman AAF, AZ	NE of Berry.
Kings Bridge, fort at, NY	Ft. Independence.
Kingsbury Battery, DC	2 mi. NE of Tennallytown.
Kingsbury, Fort, FL	St. Johns River, N side Lk. Monroe.
Kingston, Fort, PA	See Forty Fort.
Kingston, Fort, RI	Indian fort.
Kingston, Fort, UT	
Kinney Battery, NY	At Ft. Slocum.
Kinney, Fort, WY	A/k/a Ft. McKinney.
Kinsessing, Camp, IA	Near Davenport.
Kinzie, Fort, IL	
Kipp, Fort, MT	Upper Missouri River.
Kirby Battery, CA	At Ft. Baker.
Kirby Battery, SC	Near Charleston; ex-O'Rourke Battery.
Kirby Battery, MD	3 mi. above Tennallytown, DC; ex-Ft. Franklin.
Kirby, Fort, TX	On the Charceo Grande del Aqua Dulce.
Kirkwood Camp, IA	Clinton.
Kirkwood's Blockhouse, WV	Wheeling Creek, opp. Wheeling.
Kirtland AAF, NM	SE of Albuquerque.
Kissimmee AAF, FL	W of Kissimmee.
Kissimmee, Fort, FL	Kissimmee River.
Kittanning, fort at, PA	Ft. Armstrong.
Kittery Point, fort at, ME	Ft. McClary.

Klamath, Fort, OR	Lake Klamath, Klamath County.
Klock, Fort, UT	Near St. Johnsville.
Kneas, Fort, FL	Collier County, 20 mi. NE of Naples.
Knight Gen Hospital, CT	New Haven.
Kniphausen, Fort, NY	NY City.
Knollwood Field, NC	NE of Pinehurst.
Knox, Camp/Fort, KY	Hardin County.
Knox, Camp, VA	Near Alexandria.
Knox, Fort, ME	Bucksport.
Knox, Fort, IN	Vincennes.
Knoxville National Cemetery, TN	Knoxville.
Kodiak, Fort, AK	Kodiak Isl.
Kootenais, Fort, MT	Flat Bow or Kootenais River.
Korsholm, Fort, PA	
Koshkonong, Fort, WI	Lake Koshkonong.
Kouari, Fort, NY	Mohawk River, near German Flats; became known as Ft. Herkimer.
Kountz's Fort, MO	8 mi. W of St. Charles County.
Koutznou, Fort, AK	Admiralty Isl.
Krayenbuhl Battery, NJ	At Ft. Mott.
Kyle Battery, KY	At Covington.

Reminding the doughboys to write home during WWI. The scene is Fort Snelling, Minnesota.

Castle Williams, on Governor's Island, in N.Y. City's harbor, c.1893.

Gen. Robert E. Lee, CSA

Sam Houston, of Texas.

La Bay, Fort, MI	Fox River, nr. Lk, Mich., site of old Ft. Howard.
Labroarory, Camp, GA	Near Macon.
Lackawanna, Fort, PA	
Ladd Field, AK	Near Fairbanks.
La Demoiselle, Fort, OH	
Ladies Home Gen. Hospital, NY	NY City.
Lafayette Barracks, MD	Baltimore.
Lafayette, Camp, PA	At Barren Hill.
Lafayette, Camp, PA	Uniontown.
Lafayette, Fort, LA	Same as Lafitte.
Lafayette, Fort, NY	NY City harbor, at The Narrows; ex-Ft. Diamond.
Lafayette, Fort, NY	At Verplancks Point on Hudson River, opp. Stony Point.
Lafayette, Fort, PA	Pittsburgh.
Lafayette Square, Camp, MD	Baltimore.
Lafitte, Fort, LA	Grand Terre Isl., Barataria Bay.
Laidley Battery, FL	At Ft. Dade.
Laight, Fort, NY	NY City, on the heights NW of present site of Central Park.
Lajes Field, Azores	Terceira Island.
La Junta AAF, CO	NE of LaJunta.
Lake Charles AAF, CA	E of Lake Charles.
Lakeland AAF, FL	SW of Lakeland.
Lake View, Camp, MN	Lake City.
Lake Wales AAF, FL	W of Lake Wales.
Lamar, Fort, GA	Madison County.
Lamar, Fort, SC	Charleston harbor,
Lamb Battery, NC	Wilmington.
Lamb's Fort, PA	Washington County.
Lamb's Dam Battery, MA	Near Roxbury.
Lamerick, Fort, OR	
La Mott, Fort, IL	La Mott Creek.
La Motte, Fort, GA	Okeefinokee Swamp.
La Motte Island, fort on, NY	Lake Champlain, Ft. St. Anne.
Lancaster Battery, CA	At the Presidio.
Lancaster, Fort, FL	In eastern FL.
Lancaster, Fort, TX	Nr. jct. of Live Oak Creek & Pecos Riv.
Lander, Camp. ID	Snake Creek.
Landing, Fort, NC	Tyrrell County.
Lane, Fort, FL	St. Johns River, near Lake Henry.
Lane, Fort, KS	Barnesville.
Lane, Fort, NC	New Bern.
Lane, Fort, OR	8 mi. N of Jacksonville.
Lane's Fort, NC	Roanoke Island.
Langin Field, WV	Moundsville.
Langley Field, VA	3 mi. N of Hampton.
Lang Syne, Camp, FL	Near Ft. Drane.
Lapananel, Fort, PA	Philadelphia.
La Paz, Camp, AZ	Conorado Indian Reservation.
La Paz, Camp, CA	In southern California.
La Presentation, Fort, NY	Ogdensburg.

Lapwai, Fort, ID	Lapwai River, 12 mi. from Lewiston.
Laramie, Fort, MO	Linden.
Laramie, Fort, WY	Nr. mouth of Laramie River, Laramie Co.
Laramie (Loramie), Fort, OH	N part of Shelby County.
Laredo AAF, TX	NE of Laredo.
Laredo, fort at, TX	Ft. McIntosh.
La Rigolie, Fort, NY	
Larned, Fort, KS	Pawnee Fork, ex-Camp Alert.
Larrabee, Fort, ME	
La Seur (Le Seur), Fort, MN	Mississippi River, opp. mouth of the Chippewa.
Lashley's Fort, AL	Talladega.
Las Laxas, Camp, TX	On Rio Grande, 50 mi. above Ft. Ringgold.
Las Mercedes Field, Nicaragua	
Las Vegas AAF, NV	NE of Las Vegas.
Latham, Camp, CA	Near Los Angeles.
La Tour, Fort, MO	At St. Louis.
Lauderdale, Fort, FL	Head of New River Inlet, Dade Co.
Laudonniere's Camp, FL	St. Marys River.
Laughlin AAF, TX	E of Del Rio.
Laurel AAF, MS	SW of Laurel.
Laurel Hill, battery on, NY	NY City.
Laurel Hill, Fort, PA	Nr. spot later called Braddock's Grave.
Laurinburg-Maxton AAF, NC	NE of Laurinburg.
Laurens, Fort, OH	Tuscarawas River, near Bolivar.
Lavier, Fort, AL	Between Alabama & Tombigbee Rivers.
Lawn, Fort, SC	Chester County.
Lawrence, Camp, MD	Charles County.
Lawrence, Fort, GA	Flint River, 8 mi. above mouth of Patsaliga Creek.
Lawrence, Fort, NY	Brooklyn.
Lawrens Street Battery, SC	Charleston.
Lawson AAF, GA	SW of Ft. Benning.
Lawson, Camp, FL	Near Palatka.
Lawson, Camp, FL	Between St. Marks & Tallahassee.
Lawson, Camp, MS	Greenwood Isl.
Lawson, Camp, TX	75 mi. from Ft. Inge.
Lawson, Fort, GA	Near Savannah.
Lawson Gen. Hospital, MO	St. Louis.
Lawton Battery, SC	Near Savannah, GA.
Lawton, Fort, GA	" "
Lawton, Fort, WA	Magnolia Bluff, near Seattle.
Lazaretto Point, fort at, MD	Opp. Ft. McHenry, Baltimore.
Lazear Battery, MD	At Ft. Howard.
Lead Mine, Fort, PA	Foot of Bald Eagle Mtn., Huntingdon Co.
Leadville Aux. AAF, CO	NNW of Leadville.
Leavenworth Arsenal, KS	At Ft. Leavenworth.
Leavenworth, Camp, I.T. (OK)	12 mi. W of Washita.
Leavenworth, Fort, KS	3 mi. from Leavenworth City.
Leavenworth, Fort. Nat'l. Cemetery, KS	At Ft. Leavenworth.
Leavenworth Military Prison, KS	At Ft. Leavenworth.
Lebanon, Fort, PA	Susquehanna River, nr. Pt Clinton.
Lebanon National Cemetery, KY	Lebanon.
Le Boeuf, Fort, PA	Near Waterford, Erie Co.

Lechmeres Point, fort at, MA	East Cambridge.
Ledyard Battery, CA	At Ft. McDowell.
Le Dout, Fort, TX	Upper tributaries of Sabine River.
Lee Battery, WA	At Ft. Flagler.
Lee, Camp, MO	At Cowskin Prairie.
Lee, Camp, VA	Richmond.
Lee, Camp, VA	Westmoreland County.
Lee, Camp/Fort, VA	Petersburg.
Lee, Fort, GA	Savannah.
Lee, Fort, MA	At Salem Neck.
Lee, Fort, NJ	Bergen County, on Hudson River, opp. NY City at site of G. Wash. Bridge.
Lee, Fort, NC	Cape Fear River.
Lee, Fort, TN	Near Gap Creek.
Leech Lake, camp at, MN	Near Walker.
Leedy, Camp, KS	Topeka.
Leemore AAF, CA	SW of Leemore.
Leesburg AAF, FL	ENE of Leesburg.
Lee's Mills, fortifications at, VA	James River.
Legionville, Camp, PA	Ohio River, 22 mi. below Pittsburgh.
Lehigh, Fort, PA	At Lehigh Gap.
Leiter U.S. Gen. Hospital, GA	Chickamauga.
Leland, Fort, OR	
Lemhi, Fort, ID	Salmon River, Lehigh County.
Le Noult, Fort, MI	Detroit, became Ft. Shelby.
Leon, Fort, LA	
Leonard Wood, Fort, MO	St. Robert.
Leonidas, Fort, KY	
Le Seur, Fort, MN	Near Hastings, on Miss. River.
Leslie, Camp, VA	On Arlington Heights.
Les Sables, Fort, NY	Niagara River.
Letort, Fort, PA	Near Carlisle.
Levett, Fort, ME	Cushings Isl., nr. Portland.
Lewis Battery, OR	At Ft. Stevens.
Lewis, Camp, MT	Big Spring Fork of Judith River.
Lewis, Camp, OH	Pickaway County.
Lewis, Camp/Fort, WA	S of Tacoma.
Lewis, Fort, CO	Pagosa Springs, San Juan River.
Lewis, Fort, IL	
Lewis, Fort, MT	Missouri River, nr. Pablois Isl.
Lewis, Fort, NY	
Lewis, Fort, VA	Near Salem, Roanoke County.
Lewis, Fort, VA	Bath County, on Pasture River.
Lewiston, fortifications at, ME	
Lexington Aux. AAF, KY	W of Lexington.
L'Hullier, Fort, MN	Minn, River, near Lake Pepin.
Libby, Fort, MA	Gloucester.
Libby Prison, VA	Richmond.
Liberal AAF, KS	W of Liberal.
Liberty Arsenal, MO	Missouri River, Clay County.
Liberty, Fort, RI	Narragansett Bay.
Ligonier, Fort, PA	On Loyal Hanna Creek, at Ligonier.
Likens, Fort, AL	In Broom Lower Valley.
Lillie, Camp, MO	Near Jefferson City.
Lillope, Fort, PA	Wilkesboro.

Lime Point, fort at, CA	Ft. Baker.
Lincoln AAF, NE	NW of Lincoln.
Lincoln, Abe, Camp, ME	Portland.
Lincoln, Abraham, Fort, ND	See Ft. Abraham Lincoln.
Lincoln Barracks, DC	Washington.
Lincoln Battery, AL	Near Huntsville.
Lincoln Battery, FL	Santa Rosa Isl.
Lincoln Battery, GA	Tybee Island.
Lincoln, Camp, AZ	Became Ft. Verde.
Lincoln, Camp, CA	Near Crescent City.
Lincoln, Camp, MD	Baltimore.
Lincoln, Camp, MN	Lakeland.
Lincoln, Camp, MO	St. Louis.
Lincoln, Camp, VA	On the Chickahominy.
Lincoln, Fort, DC	Near Bladensburg, MD
Lincoln, Fort, KS	Osage River, 12 mi. S of Ft. Scott.
Lincoln, Fort, ND	Near Bismarck.
Lincoln, Fort, TX	On Rio Seco, 50 mi. W of San Antonio.
Lincoln Gen. Hospital, DC	Washington.
Lindley's Fort, PA	Prosperity, Washington County.
Link's Blockhouse, WV	On Middle Wheeling Creek.
Lisa, Fort, IA	Near Council Bluffs.
Liscum, Fort, AK	Port Valdez.
Litchfield, fortifications at, CT	
Little Congaree Bridge, fortifications at, SC	
Littleton (Littleton), Fort, SC	Near Beaufort.
Little Meadows, Fort, PA	
Little Rock Arsenal, AR	Little Rock, became Little Rock Barracks.
Little Rock Barracks, AR	Little Rock.
Little Rick National Cemetery, AR	" "
Little Silver Signal Corps Camp, NJ	Became Camp Alfred Vail.
Little Te,ple, fort at, LA	
Littleton, Fort, PA	Fulton County.
Liverpool Point, battery at, MD	On Potomac River.
Livingston, Camp, LA	NE of Alexandria.
Livingston, Camp, MN	Yellow Medicine.
Livingston, Fort, KY	
Livingston, Fort, LA	Grand Terre Isl., Barataria Bay.
Lloyd, Fort, FL	N of Lake Okechobee.
Lloyd Neck, fort at, NY	Northwestern Suffolk Co., Ft. Franklin.
Lobos Point, fort at, CA	Ft. Miley.
Lockbourne AAF, OH	E of Lockbourne.
Lockhaven, blockhouse at, PA	
Logan Battery, SC	At Ft. Moultrie.
Logan, Camp, OR	Strawberry Creek, Grant Co.
Logan, Camp, TX	Houston.
Logan, Fort, CO	10 mi. from Denver.
Logan, Fort, KY	Stanford, Lincoln County.
Logan, Fort, MT	In Smith River Valley, Meagher County; ex-Camp Baker.
Logan H. Roots, Fort, AT	Near Little Rock.
Logstown, Fort, PA	Ohio River.
London, Fort, PA	Franklin County.
Long Island Battery, GA	Savannah River.
Long Island, Fort, TN	Holston River.

Long Island Head, fort at, MA	Ft. Strong.
Long Point, batteries at, MA	Provincetown harbor.
Lookout, Camp, MD	Near Darnestown.
Lookout, Camp, MO	Quincy.
Lookout, Camp, SC	6 mi. from Ft. Walker.
Lookout, Camp, TN	In East Tennessee.
Lookout, Camp, VA	20 mi. from Gauley.
Lookout, Fort, SD	Missouri River, 40 mi. below Pierre.
Lookout, Fort, NC	Near Ft. Fisher.
Lookout Mtn., forts on, TN	
Lopen, Camp, TX	43 mi. from Rio Grande City.
Lopez Island Reservation, WA	San Juan County.
Loramie, Fort, OH	Darke County.
Lord Battery, SC	At Ft. Moultrie.
Loring, Camp, NM	Near Red River.
Loring Cantonment, OR	Snake River, near Ft. Hall.
Loring, Fort, MS	Leflore County.
Lorna Point Reservation, CA	San Diego harbor.
Los Cerritos, Camp, TX	Near Laredo.
Losey Field, PR	5 mi. E of Arus.
Loudon, Fort, PA	Franklin County.
Loudon, Fort, TN	Tennessee River.
Loudon, Fort, VA	Winchester.
Loudon Park National Cemetery, MD	Baltimore.
Louis, Fort, AL	Mouth of Mobile River.
Louis, Fort, IL	Ex-Ft. Crevecoeur.
Louis, Fort, RI	Narragansett Bay.
Loup River, N. Fork, post on, NE	Ft. Hartsuff.
Loups Creek Camp, VA	Near Gauley.
Louther (Lowther), Fort, PA	Carlisle.
Louverture Gen. Hospital, VA	Alexandria.
Love Field, TX	Dallas.
Lovell Gen. Hospital, RI	Portsmouth Grove.
Low, Camp, CA	San Juan.
Lowell Battery, MA	At Ft. Warren.
Lowell, Camp, VA	Prospect Hill.
Lowell, Fort, AZ	Rillito Creek, 7 mi. NE of Tucson.
Lowell, Fort, NM	Chama River, ex-Camp Plummer.
Lowell Ordnance Depot, AZ	Near Tucson.
Lowell's Island, fort on, MA	Ft. Standish.
Lower Brule Agency, fort at, ND	Ft. Hale.
Lowry Field, CO	Denver.
Lowry Point, battery at, VA	Rappahannock River.
Lowry's Fort, PA	In Canoe Valley.
Lowther Fort, PA	See Louther.
Loyal, Fort, ME	On Casco Bay.
Loyal Hanna, Fort, PA	Ligonier, Westmoreland County.
Lubbock AAF, TX	WNW of Lubbock.
Lucas' Fort, PA	Fordice.
Luke Field, AZ	N of Litchfield Park.
Luke Field, HI	Pearl Harbor.
Lukeen's Fort, AK	Near mouth of Hutituak River.
Lumberton Aux. AAF #2, NC	SW of Lumberton.
Lupton, Fort, CO	Weld County.
Lydius (Lydus), Fort, NY	Orange River.

Lyman, Fort, NY	Hudson River, nr. Lake George; became Ft. Edward.
Lynn, Fort, AR	Miller County.
Lynn Haven Bay, battery at, VA	
Lyon Battery, GA	Tybee Isl.
Lyon, Camp, ID	N fork of Jordan Creek.
Lyon, Camp, MO	At Birds Point.
Lyon, Fort, CO (first)	Arkansas River, near Bents Fort; became Ft. Wise.
Lyon, Fort, CO (second)	Arkansas River, 3 mi. below Purgatory River.
Lyon, Fort, MO	Benton County.
Lyon, Fort, NM	126 mi. NW of Albuquerque; ex-Ft. Fauntleroy.
Lyon, Fort, VA	Near Alexandria.
Lytle, Fort, PA	Huntindon County.
Lytle, Fort, TN	Chattanooga.
Lyttleton (Littleton), Fort, SC	Near Beaufort.
Lyttleton, Fort, PA	On Aughwick Creek, Northumberland Co.

Castle Clinton (a National Monument since 1946), built 1807 in NY City. By 1822, it had fallen into disuse. Shown here in 1892 as Castle Gardens, an exhibition hall and amusement palace.

N.Y. City's harbor in 1775, showing Fort George at the center.

North Battery, at the foot of Hubert Street, N.Y. City.

McAlister, Fort, PA	Cumberland County.
McAllister, Fort, GA	Great Oheechee River, near Savannah.
McAloon Battery, TN	Near Chattanooga.
McAlvey's Fort, PA	Huntingdon County.
McArthur, Camp, TX	Waco
McArthur, Fort, CA	
McArthur, Fort, OH	Scioto River, near Kenton.
McArthur, Fort, TX	
McCallister, Fort, PA	
McChord Air Field, WA	At Ft. Lewis.
McClary, Fort, ME	Kittery Point, Portsmouth harbor.
McClear, Camp, CA	Fergno River.
McClellan Battery, GA	Tybee Island.
McClellan, Camp/Fort, AL	Anniston.
McClellan, Camp, IA	Davenport.
McClellan, Camp, PA	Near Harrisburg.
McClellan, Camp, VA	Near Alexandria.
McClellan Field, CA	Sacramento.
McClellan, Fort, FL	
McClellan Gen. Hospital, PA	Nicetown.
McClelland's Fort, KY	Georgetown.
McClernand, Camp, IL	Cairo.
McCloud, Camp, TN	Near Mitchellsville.
McClure, Camp, PA	Chambersburg.
McClure, Fort, FL	Warm Springs, Withlacoochee River.
McClure. Fort, PA	Bloomsburg.
McClurg, Fort, MO	On Lime Creek.
McComb's Fort, PA	Near Doubling Gap.
McConihe Redoubt, VA	James River.
McConnell's Fort, PA	Upper Strasburg, Franklin County.
McCook AAF, NE	NNW of McCook.
McCook Field, OH	Near Dayton, became Wilbur Wright Fld.
McCook, Fort, TN	Near Battle Creek.
McCord, Fort, PA	Near Loudon.
McCorkle Battery, SC	At Ft. Moultrie.
McCormick, Fort, PA	On Stone Creek, Huntington County.
McCoy, Camp/Fort, WI	NE of Sparta.
McCoy Field, WI	SW of Camp McCoy.
McCoy, Fort, FL	Marion County.
McCoy's Fort, PA	Fayette County.
McCrabb, Fort, FL	Suwanee.
McCrary, Fort, AL	Near Roanoke.
McCulloch, Ben., Camp, MO	Near Springfield.
McDermit, Fort, NV	Quinns River, Humboldt County.
McDermitt, Fort, AL	Near Mobile.
MacDill Field, FL	Tampa.
McDonough Battery, NC	At Ft. Criswell.
McDougall Battery, NY	NY City, near Trinity Church.
McDougall Gen. Hospital, NY	At Ft. Schuyler.
McDowell, Fort, AZ	On Rio Verde, 8 mi. above jct. with Salt River.
McDowell, Fort, CA	Angel Isl., San Francisco Bay.
McDowell, Fort, PA	Franklin County.

McElery's Fort, PA — On Shavers Creek.
McFarland Battery, MD — At Ft. Armistead.
McFarland, Fort, PA — Washington County.
McGarry, Camp, NV — At Summit Springs, Lassen County.
McGees Station, KY — N of Kentucky River.
McGilvery, Fort, VA — Near Petersburg.
McGinnis, Camp, TN — Fentress County.
McGowans Pass, fortifications at, NY
McGrath Battery, CA — At Ft. Rosecrans.
Machault, Fort, PA — Franklin.
McHenry, Fort, MD — Baltimore.
McHenry, Fort, WY
Machias, fortifications at, ME
McIntosh Battery, AL — Near Mobile.
McIntosh Battery, FL — At Ft. Dade.
McIntosh, Fort, GA — Saltilla River.
McIntosh, Fort, PA — Mouth of Beaver Creek, 20 mi. from Pittsburgh.
McIntosh, Fort, TX — On Rio Grande, near Laredo; ex-Camp Crawford.
Mackall, Camp, CA — In Round Valley.
McKavett Battery, NC — At Ft. Caswell.
McKavett, Fort, TX — Menard Co., 2 mi. from source of San Saba River.
McKay (Mackay), Fort, FL — Ocklawaha River.
Mackay, Fort, KS — Arkansas River.
McKay, Fort, WI — Prairie du Chien.
McKean, Camp, IA — Near Mt. Pleasant.
McKean, Fort, NE — Became Ft. McPherson.
McKean, Fort, NY — 56 mi. W of Albany.
McKean, Fort, ND — Became Ft. Abraham Lincoln.
McKee, Camp, AZ — Ex-Ft. Mason.
McKee, Camp, NE — On Granite Creek.
McKee's Fort, PA — Dauphin Co., nr. McKee's Falls.
McKellar Field, TN — SW of Jackson.
Mackenzie, Camp, GA — Augusta.
Mackenzie, Fort, WY — Near Sheridan.
Mackeys Island, camp on, ME — Portland harbor.
McKim, Camp, MD — Baltimore.
McKim's Mansion Gen. Hospital, MD — "
Mackinac, Fort, MI — Mackinac Isl.
McKinley, Camp, HI — Honolulu.
McKinley, Camp, IA — Des Moines.
NcKinley, Fort, ME — Great Diamond Isl., Portland Harbor.
McKinley's Blockhouse, KY
McKinney, Fort, WY — Powder River; ex-Cantonment Reno.
Mackintosh Redoubt, AL — Near Mobile.
McKinzie, Fort, MT
McKown, Camp, WI — 35 mi. N of Madison.
McLane, Camp, PA — Near Erie.
McLane, Fort, GA — Okeefinokee Swamp.
McLane, Fort, NM — 15 mi. S of Santa Rita copper mines.
McLean Battery, KY — Near Newport.
McLemore, Camp, FL — Withlacoochee River.
McLouis, Fort, MO — Near site of New Franklin. See Ft. Hempstead.

McMahon, Fort, VA	Near Petersburg.
McNeill, Fort, FL	Near Lake Poinsett.
Macomb, Fort, FL #1	Suwanee River, Lafayette County.
Macomb, Fort, FL #2	St, Marks River, 10 mi. N of St. Marks.
Macomb, Fort, LA	Chef Menteur Pass; ex-Ft. Wood.
Macon, Fort, NC	Bogue Isl., Beaufort harbor.
McPherson, Camp, AZ	Became Camp Date Creek.
McPherson, Fort/Barracks. GA	Atlanta.
McPherson, Fort, KY	Near Louisville.
McPherson, Fort, MS	Natchez.
McPherson, Fort, NE	Cottonwood Springs; ex-Cantonment McKean.
McPherson, Fort, VA	Near Arlington.
McPherson, Fort, Nat'l. Cemetery, NE	Maxwell, Lincoln County.
McPherson Gen. Hospital, MS	Vicksburg.
McRae Battery, KY	Near Ft. Mitchell.
McRae, Fort, FL	Near Lake Okeechobee.
McRae, Fort, NM	Nr. Rio Grande, at the Ojo del Muerto.
McRae, Fort, VA	Near Poplar Grove Church.
McRee, Fort, FL	Pensacola Bay, opp. Ft. Pickens.
McReynolds, Camp, PA	Philadelphia.
Madison AAF, KY	NW of Madison.
Madison Barracks, NY	At Sacket Harbor.
Madison Battery, NC	At Ft. Caswell.
Madison, Camp, KY	Franklin County.
Madison, Fort, AL	Between Alabama & Tombigbee Rivers.
Madison, Fort, IL	Mississippi River, near Bellview.
Madison, Fort, IA	Lee County.
Madison, Fort, ME	Castine.
Madison, Fort, MD	Annapolis.
Madison, Fort, MS	
Madison, Fort, SC	Oconee County.
Madras AAF, OR	NNW of Madras.
Maggofin, Camp, NM	Near White Mountain.
Maginnis, Fort, MT	Gergus Co., 53 mi. from Rocky Point.
Magnolia Bluff, fort at, WA	Ft. Lawton.
Magruder, Camp, KS	Arkansas River.
Magruder, Fort, VA	Near Williamsburg.
Mahan, Battery, NY	At Ft. Totten.
Mahan, Fort, DC	Near Washington.
Mahone, Fort, VA	Near Petersburg.
Maine, Camp, NY	NY City.
Maine Island Reservation, CA	San Pablo Bay.
Maison Blanche Field, Algeria	
Maitland, Fort, FL	Near Lake Monroe.
Majors Field, TX	E of Caddo Mills.
Malade, Fort, ID	Malade River.
Malden AAF, MD	NNW of Malden.
Mallory, Fort, TN	At Cumberland Gap.
Mamacock, Fort, CT	New London.
Manada, Fort, PA	Dauphin County.
Manainung, Fort, PA	At mouth of Schuylkill.
Manary's Blockhouse, OH	86 mi. from Chillicothe.
Manchac, Fort, LA	Mississippi River, nr. Baton Rouge.
Manchester, blockhouse at, OH	

Mandan, Fort, ND	On Missouri River.
Manhattan Island, forts on, NY	NY City.
Manhattanville, redoubts at, NY	Bronx County.
Mann, Fort, KS	8 mi. from Dodge City.
Mansfield, blockhouse at, OH	
Mansfield, Camp, LA	Carrollton.
Mansfield, Camp, AZ	7 mi. S of Ft. Defiance.
Mansfield, Fort, MD	Near Tennallytown.
Mansfield Gen. Hospital, NC	Moorehead.
Mantanzas, Fort, FL	Anastasia Isl.
Manuel's Fort, MT	Yellowstone River, at mouth of the Big Horn River.
Many, Fort, FL	16 mi. SE of Tallahassee.
Marana AAF, AZ	NW of Marana.
Marblehead Arsenal, MA	Marblehead.
March Field, CA	Riverside.
Marcy, Fort, NM	Santa Fe.
Marcy, Fort, NY	
Marcy, Fort, TX	Bear Corpus Christi.
Marcy, Fort, CA	Near Chain Bridge.
Marcus Hook, Fort, PA	Delaware River, 18 mi. SW of Phila.
Marfa AAF, TX	SW of Marfa.
Marfa Aux. Field, TX	N of Marfa.
Marfa, Camp, TX	Marfa.
Margarets, Fort, OH	Hocking River.
Marian Islands Reservation, CA	San Francisco harbor.
Marianna AAF, FL	NE of Marianna.
Marianna, fort at, FL	
Marietta AAF, GA	SE of Marietta.
Marietta, fortifications at, OH	
Marietta National Cemetery, GA	Near Marietta.
Marine Gen. Hospital, LA	New Orleans.
Marine Gen. Hospital, MO	St. Louis.
Marine Gen. Hospital, OH	Cincinnati.
Marion Battery, SC	Sullivans Island.
Marion, Camp, SC	Summerville.
Marion Branch Bat'l. Mil. Home, IN	Grant County.
Marion, Camp. VA	At Uptons Hill.
Marion, Fort, FL	St. Augustine, a/k/a Ft. San Marcos & Castle of St. Mark.
Marion, Fort, SC	Beaufort.
Marshall Battery, VA	Near Richmond.
Marshall, Camp, WY	N Fork of Platte River.
Marshall, Fort, MD	Baltimore.
Marshall, Fort, SC	Sullivans Isl.
Marshall's Fort, PA	Washington County.
Martello Tower, FL	Key West.
Martello Tower, LA	Bayou Bienvenue.
Martello Tower, Fort, SC	Sullivans Isl.
Martin, Fort, PA	Bedford County.
Martin's Fort, KY	Licking River.
Martin's Fort, WV	Crooked River, Monongalia County.
Martin Scott, Fort, TX	On a branch of the Colorado, near Fredericksburg.

Mary, Fort, ME	Biddeford.
Maryville AAF, CA	E of Maryville.
Mason, Camp, TX	On the Limpia,
Mason, Fort, AZ	12 mi. SE of Tubac; became Ft. McKee.
Mason, Fort, CA	At Black Point, San Francisco.
Mason, Fort, FL	Nr. St. Johns River, 14 mi. SW of Volusia.
Mason, Fort, MO	Miss. River, 100 mi. N of St. Louis.
Mason, Fort, TX	Comanche Creek, near the Llano River.
Mason's Fort, PA	Fayette County.
Masonic Hall, fortifications at, MO	Near Lexington.
Masonic Redoubt, NY	At Brooklyn.
Massac, Fort, IL	Ohio River, 11 mi. below Paducah, KY.
Massachusetts Battery, VA	At Suffolk.
Massachusetts, Camp, VA	Alexandria.
Massachusetts, Fort, CO	Utah Creek, 2 mi. from Ft. Garland.
Massachusetts, Fort, DC	Nr. Washington; became Ft. Stevens.
Massachusetts, Fort, MA	Hoosic River.
Massachusetts, Fort, MS	Ship Island.
Massachusetts State Soldiers' Home, MA	Chelsea.
Matagorda Bay, battery at, TX	Matagorda Bay.
Matagorda Island, fort on, TX	Ft. Esperanza.
Matagorda Island Gunnery Range Field, TX	Eastern Matagorda Isl.
Matagorda Peninsula Field, TX	Matagorda Peninsula.
Matamoras, camp at, Mexico.	Became Ft. Brown.
Matanzas Inlet, Fort, FL	
Mathias, Point, battery at, VA	Lower Potomac River.
Matheo, Fort, FL	See San Matheo.
Mather Field, CA	12 mi. SE of Sacramento.
Mathews, Fort, GA	
Matson, Fort, MO	
Matthews, Fort, FL	Oconee River.
Maui Field, HI	Maui Isl.
Maverick's Fort, MA	
Maxey, Fort, NY	On Blackwell's Isl.
Maxwell AAF, AL	W of Montgomery.
Maxwell's Fort, PA	Conococheague Creek.
Meade, Camp, PA	Middletown.
Meade, Fort, FL	Pease Creek, Polk Co.
Meade, Fort/Field, MD	Baltimore.
Meade, Fort, SD	Bear Bute Creek, nr. Sturgis; ex-Camp Ruhlen.
Meagher, Camp, DC	Near Washington.
Means, Fort, GA	
Mears, Fort, AK	
Mechanic, Fort, SC	Charleston.
Medford Army Air Base, OR	Medford.
Medicine Butte, Camp, WY	Near Evanston.
Medill, Camp, OR	Grove Creek.
Meeks Field, Iceland	
Meigs Battery, MD	At Ft. Washington.
Meigs, Camp, MA	Readville.

Meigs, Camp, PA	Philadelphia.
Meigs, Fort, OH	At the Rapids of the Maumee.
Meigs, Fort, NY	
Meigs, Fort, DC	E of the Eastern Branch.
Meikle, Fort, VA	Petersburg.
Meiklejohn, Camp, NE	Omaha.
Mellon, Fort, FL	Lake Monroe.
Memphis, fort at, TN	Ft. Pickering.
Memphis National Cenetery, TN	Memphis.
Mendocino, fort at, CA	Ft. Bragg.
Menlendael, Fort, PA	Near Philadelphia.
Menninger, Fort, PA	Nr. mouth of Warrior Run.
Merced AAF, CA	NW of Merced.
Mercer, Fort, NJ	Delaware River, opp. Ft. Mifflin.
Meredith, Camp, PA	Near Greencastle.
Merriam, Camp, CA	At the Presidio.
Merrill Battery, LA	At Ft. St. Philip.
Merrill, Fort, TX	Neuces River, 50 mi. NW of Corpus Christi.
Merritt, Camp, CA	At the Presidio.
Merritt, Camp, MT	At Tongue River Agency.
Mexico City National Cemetery, Mexico	Mecico City, DF
Miami, Fort, MI	Mouth of Josephs River.
Miami, Fort, MO	Missouri River, just below Ft, Osage.
Miami, Fort, IN	Later the site of Ft. Wayne.
Miamie, Fort, OH	Maumee River.
Miamis, Fort, IL	Illinois River.
Micanopy, Fort, FL	Micanopy.
Michael, Fort, AK	Michael Isl.
Michalotzky, Fort, TN	Nr. Chattanooga.
Michault, Fort, PA	French Creek.
Michie, Fort, NY	Great Gull Isl., 12 mi. below New London, CT.
Michigan, Camp, MD	Annapolis.
Michigan State Soldiers' Home, MI	Grand Rapids.
Michilimackinac Island, fort on, MI	Ft. Mackinac.
Middle Ground, fort on, NY	NY City harbor.
Middleton, Fort, IL	Kaskaskia River.
Midland AAF, TX	SW of Midland.
Midway, fort at, GA	
Mifflin, Fort, PA	Mud Island, Delaware River, 7 mi. from Philadelphia.
Mike, Fort, CA	Point Lobis, San Francisco harbor.
Mile 26 Field, AK	Fairbanks; satellite of Ladd Field.
Miley, Fort, CA	
Milford, Indian fortifications at, CT	York County.
Mill, Fort, SC	Okefinokee Swamp.
Millar, A.S., Fort, GA	Near Dalton.
Millar Battery, LA	At Ft. Jackson.
Mill Creek, works on, GA	
Mill Creek, Redoubt, NC	Plymouth.
Millen Prison, GA	Millen.
Miller, Camp, CA	At the Presidio.

Miller, Camp, MO	Became Jefferson Barracks.
Miller, Field, NY	New Dorp, Staten Island.
Miller, Fort, CA	San Joaquin River, at Millerton.
Miller, Fort, MA	Nangus Head, Salem harbor,
Miller, Fort, NY	Washington County.
Miller, Silas, Camp, KY	Green River.
Miller's Blockhouse, PA	Hannastown.
Mill Farm, Camp, KY	Lexington.
Milliken, Fort, PA	Washington County.
Millrock, fort at, NY	East River, at mouth of Harlem River, NY City.
Mills, Camp, NY	Nassau County.
Mills, Camp, TN	Near Paris.
Mills, Fort, FL	10 mi. from Newnansville.
Mills, Fort, Philippines	Corregidor Island
Mill Springs National Cemetery, KY	Mill Springs.
Mims, Fort, AL	Near Montgomery.
Minnesota State Soldiers' Home, MN	Minnehaha.
Minnisink, Fort, NY	Orange County.
Minter Field, CA	NW of Bakersfield.
Miro, Fort, FL	Washita River, about 100 mi. above its mouth.
Miskatonic Field, MA	
Misery, Camp, VA	Near Martinsburg.
Mississippi, Fort, LA	Poverty Point, 38 mi. below New Orleans.
Missoula, Fort, MT	Bitter Root River, 4 mi. from Missoula Station.
Missouri Battery, AL	Above Dog River, nr. Spanish Fort.
Missouri Ordnance Depot, Liberty Arsenal, MO	
Missouri State Soldier's Home, MO	St. James, MO
Mitchel Field, NY	Mineola, Nassau County.
Mitchell Aux. AAF, SD	N of Mitchell.
Mitchell Battery, RI	At Ft. Greble.
Mitchell, Camp/Fort, KY	Near Covington.
Mitchell, Camp, NE	Jct. of Spoon Hill Creek & N Fork of Platte River.
Mitchell, Camp, TN	Nashville.
Mitchell, Fort, AL	Russell Co., Chattahoochee River, 10 mi. below Columbus.
Mitchell, Fort, FL	Tenhallama River.
Mitchell, Fort, GA	Chattahoochee River.
Mitchell, Fort, VA	Lunenburg County.
Mobile National Cemetery, AL	Near Mobile.
Mobile Point, forts at, AL	Fts. Morgan & Seraf.
Moccasin Point, fort at, TN	Tennessee River.
Modesto Aux. Field, CA	SE of Modesto.
Moffit Channel, battery at, SC	Sullivans Isl.
Mogollon, Camp, AZ	Became Ft. Apache.
Mohawk Castle, Fort, NY	Danube.
Mohawk River, camp on, NY	Mouth of Mohawk.
Mohican, Fort, NY	Near Manhattan.
Mojave, Fort, AZ	Colorado River, near the head of Mojave Valley.
Molate Island Reservation, CA	San Francisco Bay.
Monets Bluff, fortifications at, LA	Cane River.

97

Moniac, Fort, FL	At Hogans Ferry, on St Marys River.
Monks Corner, camp at, SC	30 mi. N of Charleston.
Monmouth Court House, camp at, NJ	
Monmouth, Fort, NJ	Oceanport; ex-Camp Alfred Vail.
Monroe Arsenal, Fort, VA	At Ft. Monroe.
Monroe, Camp, ND	Red River, opp. Pembina.
Monroe, Camp, FL	Became Ft. Mellon.
Monroe, Camp, OR	Near Cincinnati.
Monroe, Fort, VA	At Old Point Comfort.
Montana State Soldiers' Home, MT	Columbia Falls.
Montbrook AAF, FL	S of Williston.
Monteil Battery, NC	Roanoke Isl.
Monterey Barracks, CA	Monterey.
Monterey, Fort, CA	"
Monterey Ordnance Depot, CA	"
Monterey, Redoubt. CA	"
Montgomery Battery, VA (2nd)	At Ft. Monroe.
Montgomery Battery, VA (1st)	Near Suffolk.
Montgomery, Camp, PA	Near Pittsburgh.
Montgomery, Fort, AL	Nr. Alabama River, opp. the "Cut Off."
Montgomery, Fort, CA	Near San Francisco.
Montgomery, Fort, FL	5 mi. NW of Pensacola.
Montgomery, Fort, MS	
Montgomery, Fort, NY (1st)	Hudson River, 6 mi. S of West Point.
Montgomery, Fort, NY (2nd)	Rouses Point.
Montgomery, Fort, NC	Cherokee County.
Moody Field, GA	S of Barretts.
Moon Battery, NY	
Moore, Camp, AZ	Became Ft. Buchanan.
Moore, Camp, KY	Near Columbus.
Moore, Camp, LA	Near Tangipahoa.
Moore, Camp, MS	Near Corinth.
Moore, Fort, GA	At Allatoona Pass.
Moore, Fort, SC	Savannah River, 120 mi. from Charleston.
Moore Island, fort on, ME	Ft. Sullivan.
Moores Creek Bridge, works at, NC	
Moorestown Field, NJ	N of Moorestown.
Moosa, Fort, FL	Near St. Augustine.
Moosoonee Field, Canada	James Bay, Quebec.
Mora River, fort on, NM	Ft. Union.
Moreau, Fort, NY	Near Plattsburgh.
Moreno Point Reservation, FL	Entrance to Santa Rosa Sound.
Morgan, Cantonment, FL	Cedar Keys.
Morgan, Camp, FL	Pensacola,
Morgan, Fort, AL	Mobile Point, E side entrance to Mobile Bay.
Morgan, Fort, CO	S Fork of Platte River, Morgan Co; ex-Camp Wardwell.
Morgan, Fort, MS	Davis Mills.
Morgan, Fort, NC	S side of Ocracoke Inlet.
Morgantown, fort at, WV	
Morris Battery, DC	Near Washington.
Morris, Camp, CA	San Bernardino.
Morris, Camp, FL	Lake Topopekaliga.
Morris, Fort, GA	Sunbury.
Morris, Fort, PA	Shippensburg.

Morris, Fort, VA	Near Richmond.
Morris, Fort, WV	E of Uniontown.
Morris Island, works on, SC	
Morrison Field, FL	Near West Palm Beach.
Morrisons Fort, MA	Colerain, Franklin Co.
Morristown, Camp at, NJ	
Morrow, Fort, AK	Near Bristol Bay.
Morrow, Fort, GA	
Morse Field, HI	
Morton Battery, AL	Near Ft. Morgan.
Morton Battery, NY	At Ft. Wadsworth, Staten Island.
Morton, Camp, IN	Near Indianapolis.
Morton, Fort, TN	Nashville.
Morton, Fort, VA	2 mi. from Georgetown, DC.
Morton, Fort, VA	Near Petersburg.
Morton, St. Clair, Fort, KY	Louisville.
Mosby, Camp, TX	San Antonio.
Moschelosburg, Fort, NJ	See Elfsborg & Elsinburg.
Mose, Fort, FL	See Ft. Moosa.
Moses Creek, camp at, NY	Hudson River, 5 mi. from Ft. Edward.
Moses Lake Aux. AAF, WA	NNW of Neppel.
Mott, Fort, NJ	At Finns Point.
Mott, Fort, VT	Pittsford; a/k/a Ft. Vengeance.
Motte, Fort, SC	Orangeburg County.
Moulder, Camp, FL	At Pavillion Keys.
Moultrie Aux. Field, GA	S of Moultrie.
Moultrie, Fort, FL	Near St. Augustine.
Moultrie, Fort, SC	Sullivans Isl, Charleston harbor.
Mound Battery, AL	Near Mobile.
Mound Battery, NC	Near Ft. Fisher.
Mound City National Cemetery, IL	Mound City.
Mount, Camp, IN	Indianapolis.
Mountain, Fort, GA	Murray County.
Mountain Home AAF, ID	SW of Mountain Home.
Mount Clemens Aviation Camp, MI	Mount Clemens.
Mount Defiance, Fort, NY	Near Ticonderoga.
Mount Desert, fort at, ME	
Mount Hope Battery, NY	At Mount Hope.
Mount Idaho, reservation at, ID	
Mount Independence, fort on, NY	Near Lake Champlain.
Mount Independence, fort on, NY	Ft. Putnam, West Point.
Mount Malady, Fort, VA	Henrico.
Mount Pleasant, Fort, PA	
Mount Pleasant Gen. Hospital, DC	Washington.
Mount Pleasant, fort at, MD	Ft. Cumberland.
Mount Pleasant Battery, SC	Sullivans Isl.
Mount Vernon Arsenal, AL	Mt. Vernon.
Mount Vernon Barracks, AL	" "
Mount Vernon Battery, VA	At Ft. Hunt, Potomac River.
Mount Washington, fortifications at, PA	Pittsburgh.
Mowdey Battery, VA	Near Suffolk.
Mower Gen. Hospital, PA	West Philadelphia.
Muckleshute, Camp, WA	On Muckleshute Prairie, White River.
Mud Battery, GA	Near Savannah.

Mud, Fort, NY	Sacket Harbor.
Mud, Fort, OH	Near Springfield.
Mud, Fort, TX	Near mouth of Red River.
Mud Island, Fort on, PA	Ft. Mifflin, Delaware River.
Mudge Battery, MD	At Ft. Armistead.
Mudge, Fort, GA	Nr. Okeefinokee Swamp, 9 mi. from Floyd.
Mueller, Camp, MN	New Ulm.
Mulberry Point, fort at, VA	James River, near Richmond.
Mulgrave, Fort, CA	
Mull, Fort, NY	
Mulley Key, fort at, FL	Ft. De Soto.
Muncy, Fort, PA	Pennsburg.
Munsons Hill, Fort on, VA	Ft. Skedaddle, 1 mi. S of Falls Church.
Murfreesboro, camp at, TN	
Muroc AAF, CA	8 mi. W of Boron.
Murray, Camp, UT	Near Peoa, 40 mi. from Salt Lk. City.
Murray, Camp, WA	Ft. Lewis.
Musa (Muse), Fort, FL	See Ft. Moosa.
Muschestosburg, Fort, NJ	See Elfsborg & Elsinburg.
Musgroves Mills, post at, SC	Enoree River.
Myakka, Fort, FL	Myakka River, 40 mi. SE of Tampa.
Myer, Fort, VA	Arlington, on site of old Ft. Whipple.
Myers, Camp, KY	Overton County.
Myers, Fort, FL	Caloosahatchee Rver, on site of old Ft. Harvie.
Myerstown, Fort at, PA	
Myrtle Beach AAF, SC	SW of Myrtle Beach.
Mystic, Fort, CT	Mystic River.
Mystic, Fort, RI	

Nacogdoches, Fort, TX	Nacogdoches.
Nahucke, Fort, NC	Greene County.
Naknek Air Base, AK	
Nangus Head, fort at, MA	Ft. Miller.
Nansemond, Fort, VA	Near Suffolk.
Nantasket Head, fort at, MA	Ft. Revere.
Napatree Point, fort at, RI	Ft. Mansfield.
Napier Field, AL	NW of Grimes.
Narragansett, Fort, RI	Near site of Kingston.
Narrowstone Point Reservation, WA	Entrance to Port Townsend.
Naseway Shoals, fort at, VA	
Nash, Fort, TN	Head of Nortons Creek, NE of Shelbyville.
Nashborough, Fort, TN	Now Nashville.
Nashville National Cemetery, TN	Nashville.
Nassau, Fort, NJ	Opp. Philadelphia.
Nassau, Fort, NY	Castle Island, Hudson River.
Natchez National Cemetery, MS	Natchez.
Natchez, Fort, MS (#1)	Near Natchez.
Natchez, Fort, MS (#2)	On Washita & Little Rivers.
Natchitoches, fort at, LA	Ft. Claiborne.
Nath. Greene, Fort, RI	Narragansett.
National Hotel Gen. Hospital, MD	Baltimore.
Neah Bay Reservation, WA	Near Cape Flattery.
Neally, Fort, WV	N of Martinsburg.
Nebraska State Soldiers' Homes, NE	Grand Island & Milford.
Necessity, Fort, OH	Near Scioto River, Hardin County.
Necessity, Fort, LA	Franklin Co., 20 mi. S of Winnsboro.
Necessity, Fort, PA	At the Great Meadows, Fayette Co.
Neeches, Fort, TX	River Neches.
Neck, Fort, NY	Long Island.
Needles AAF, CA	S of Needles.
Negas, Fort, ME	Penobscot River.
Negley, Camp, KY	Near Nolin River.
Negley, Camp, MD	Near Hagerstown.
Negley, Fort, TN	Chattanooga.
Negley, Fort, TN	Nashville.
Negleys Hill, fortifications, PA	Near Pittsburgh.
Negro, Fort, FL	Apalachicola River.
Negro, Fort, NY	In SW part of state.
Neils Station, WV	On the Kanawha, near Parkersburg.
Neilson, Fort, NY	Near Bemis Heights.
Nellis Field, NV	8 mi. W of Las Vegas.
Nelson, Camp, KY	Near Hickman's bridge.
Nelson, Camp, National Cemetery, KY	At Camp Nelson.
Nelson, Fort, KY	Louisville.
Nelson, Fort. VA	W side Norfolk harbor, opp. Ft. Norfolk.
Nelson Gen. Hospital, KY	At Camp Nelson.
Nesqually, Fort, WA	Nesqually River.
Neutral Island, fort on, ME	
Nevills Spring, Camp at, TX	Near Ft. Davis.
Nevin, Camp, KY	9 mi. below Elizabethtown.
New Albany National Cemetery, IN	New Albany.
New Amstel, Fort, DE	New Castle (See Niewar Amstel).

New Bedford AAF, MA	N of New Bedford.
New Bedford, fortifications at, MA	
New Bern National Cemetery, NC	New Bern.
Newberry's blockhouse, OH	Below Belpre.
New Brighton, blockhouse at, PA	New Brighton.
Newburyport, defenses at, MA	
New Casco, Fort, ME	Presumpscot River.
New Castle AAF, DE	S of Wilmington.
New Castle Arsenal, DE	New Castle.
New Cumberland Army Depot, PA	Near Harrisburg.
New Dartmouth, fort at, ME	
New Dungeness Harbor, reservation at, WA	
New Gloucester, blockhouse at, ME	
New Guttenburg, Fort, DE	Timicum Isl.
New Hackensack AAF, NY	NE of Wappingers Falls.
New Hampshire State Sioldiers Home, NH	Tilton.
New Haven AAF, CT	SE of New Haven.
New Haven, fort at, VT	
New Hope, Camp, FL	In E Florida.
New Inverness, fort at, GA	
New Jersey State Soldiers' Homes, NJ	Kearney & Vineland.
New Madrid, Fort, MO	Near New Madrid.
New Orleans Arsenal, LA	New Orleans.
New Orleans Barracks, LA	Became Jackson Barracks.
Newport AAF, AR	NE of Newport.
Newport Arsenal, KY	Newport.
Newport Barracks, KY	"
Newport, Fort, NY	Near Mohawk River.
Newport Harbor, defenses of, RI	
Newport News, fort at, VA	Ft. Butler.
Newton, Camp, VA	Fairfax County.
Newton, Camp, VA	Westpoint.
Newton, Fort, NY	Staten Isl., at Ft. Wadsworth.
Newton University Gen. Hospital, MD	Baltimore.
Newtown, fort at, NY	
New Utrecht Point, fort at, NY	
New York Arsenal, NY	Governors Isl., NY City harbor.
New York Port of Embarkation, NY	NY City.
New York State Soldiers' Homes, NY	Bath & Oxford.
Nez Perce, Fort, WA	Became Ft. Walla Walla.
Niagara Fort, NY	Mouth of Niagara, 1 mi. from Youngstown.
Nicholas, Fort, AK	Cook River.
Nichols, Camp/Field, Philippines	Rizal Province.
Nichols, Fort, I.T., (OK)	15 mi. from Boise City.
Nichols, Fort, MA	Salisbury Point, opp. Newburyport.
Nicholson, Battery, MD	At Ft. Howard.
Nicholson, Fort, NY	Hudson River, nr. Lake George; supposed to be same as Ft. Edward.
Niewar Amstel, Fort, DE	New Castle (See New Amstel).
Ninety-six, Fort, SC	Near Cambridge, Abbeyville area.
Niobrara, Fort, NE	Cherry Co., on Niobrara River, opp. mouth of Minnichudza River.
Noble, Battery, TN	Near Knoxville.
Noble, Camp, IN	Near New Albany.
Noddles Island, fort on, MA	Boston harbor.

Noel, Fort, FL	8 mi. NE of Perry, Taylor Co.
Nogales, Fort, MS	Miss. River, at Walnut Hills.
Nome Air Base, AK	Nome.
Nominac, Fort, PA	W bank of Delaware River.
Nonsense, Fort, CT	Near New London, a/k/a Ft. Folly.
Nonsense, Fort, NJ	Near Morristown.
Nooks Hill, fortifications on, MA	Near Boston.
Norembega, Fort, ME	Penobscot River.
Norfolk, Fort, VA	1 mi. N of Norfolk.
Normandy, blockhouse at, TN	
Normoyle, Camp, TX	San Antonio.
Norridgewock, Fort, ME	
Norris, Fort, PA	Lehigh River, nr. Stroudsburg.
North, Battery, MA	
North, Battery, NY	At Ft. Mitchie.
North Battery, NY	NY City, foot of Hubert Street.
Northampton, fortifications at, MA	
North Bend, blockhouse at, OH	
North Carolina Arsenal, NC	Fayetteville.
North Castle, fortifications, NY	
North Cliff, Battery, NY	
North Dakota State Soldiers' Home, ND	Lisbon.
North Edisto Inlet, fortifications on, SC	
North Island Reservation, CA	San Diego harbor.
Northern, Camp, GA	Griffin.
Northfield, fortifications, MA	
North Fork of the Canadian, cantonment on, I.T. (OK)	
North Hero, blockhouse at, VT	At Dutchmans Point.
North Island, fort on, ME	
Northkill, fort, PA	2 mi. from Strausstown, Berks Co.
North Point, Battery, RI	Narragansett Bay.
North Point, fort at, MD	Ft. Howard.
Northport, fortification at, NY	Eatons Neck, entr. to Northport Bay.
North River, battery on, NY	NY City.
North Santee, redoubt on, SC	Mouth of N. Santee River.
Northwestern Branch National Home, WI	Milwaukee Co.
North Yarmouth, stockades at, ME	Royal River.
Norton, Fort, GA	22 mi. SE from Ft. Floyd.
Norton's blockhouse, OH	
Nugen, Fort, WA	Whidbys Isl.
Nuke Hill, fortifications on, MA	Near Boston.
Nulato, Fort, AK	Yukon River.
Nutter's Battery, NY	Near McGowans Pass.
Nutter's Fort, WV	
Nye, Camp, NV	Near Carson City.

Oak Creek, fort on, TX	Ft. Chadbourne.
Oak Island, fort on, NC	Ft. Caswell.
Oakland, Fort, FL	5 mi. from Ft. Doane.
Oak Point, Fort, NC	Wilmington.
Oblong Redoubt, NY	Near West Point.
O'Brien, Fort, ME	
Observation, Camp, MD	Near Poolesville.
Ocilla, Fort, FL	Between Ocilla & Wacissa Rivers.
Ocklawaha, Fort, FL	Near Apalachicola.
Ocklockony River, fort at, NC	Ft. Morgan.
Ocmulgee, Fort, GA	
Offutt Field, NE	S of Omaha.
Ogden, Battery, RI	At Ft. Greble.
Ogden, Fort, FL	De Soto Co., nr. Pease River.
Ogeechee, Fort, GA	Near Ogeechee River.
Oglethorpe Barracks, GA (original)	St. Simons Isl.
Oglethorpe Barracks, GA (later)	Savannah.
Oglethorpe, Fort, GA	"
Ohio Falls, fort at, IN	Opp. Louisville, KY.
Ohio State Soldiers' Home, OH	Sandusky.
Ojo Caliente, camp at, NM	An outpost of Ft. Craig.
Okanagon, Fort, WA	Jct. of Columbia & Okanagon Rivers.
Olden, Camp, NJ	Trenton.
Old Gate Gen Hospital, TN	Memphis.
Old Point Comfort, fort at, VA	Ft. Monroe.
Old State Gen. Hospital, TN	Memphis, TN
Old Tappan, cantonment at, NJ	
Old Topsail Inlet, Fort, NC	See Topsail Inlet, old.
Old Tower, GA	Tybee Isl.
Olive Bend Creek Stockade, OH	Near Waterford.
Olmstead, Camp, VA	Near Falls Church.
Olmstead Field, PA	Middletown.
Olmus, Camp, TX	Near San Antonio.
Olney, Stephen, Camp, SC	Hilton Head.
Olympia AAF, WA	S of Olympia.
Olympia, Camp, VT	Burlington.
Omaha Barracks/Fort, NE	Omaha.
O'Meary, Lunette, TN	Chattanooga.
One, Number, Aux. AAF, NC	At Ft. Bragg.
One, Number, Battery, VA	Wormsley Creek.
One, Number, Battery, KY	Near Island #10.
One, Number, Fort, FL	11 mi. from Indian River.
One, Number, Fort. GA	Near Savannah.
One, Number, Fort, MA	Charles River.
Oneida, fort at, NY	Ft. Bull.
Onion River, fort on, VT	Ft. Frederick.
Onondaga, Battery, VA	
Ontario AAF, CA	E of Ontario.
Ontario, Fort, NY	Oswego, site of old Ft. Pepperell.
Onward, Camp, GA	Savannah.
Onyades, Fort, NY	
Opelika, Fort, AL	Opelika.
Oplandt, Fort, NJ	Near Lewiston.

Orange County AAF, CA	NE of Costa Mesa.
Orange, Fort, NY (#1)	Bowling Green, NY City.
Orange, Fort, NY (#2)	Albany.
Ord, Camp, AZ	Became Ft. Apache.
Ord, Fort, CA	Monterey Peninsula.
Oregon, Fort, NC	Ocracoke Inlet.
Oregon State Soldiers' Home, OR	Roseburg.
Orford, Fort, OR	Port Orford.
Orleans, Fort, MO	Near mouth of the Osage.
O'Rourke, Battery, SC	Morris Isl.
O'Rourke, Fort, VA	Near Washington, DC.
Oroville AAF, CA	SW of Oroville.
Osao, Fort, NY	Missouri River, nr. later site of Sibley.
Osborne, Camp, ID	Osburn.
Osceola, Battery, FL	At Key West.
Osceola, Fort, AR	Plum Point, Mississippi River.
Oscoda AAF, WI	NW of Oscoda.
Osoyoos, Camp, WA	Lake Osoyoos, Okinakane Valley.
Ossabaw Sound, fortifications at, GA	
Ossipee, fort at, NH	
Oswegatchie, Fort, NY	Near Ogdensburg.
Oswego, Fort, NY	Later site of Ft. Ontario; ex-Ft. Pepperell.
Otis, Camp, HI	Honolulu.
Otis Field, MA	At Camp Edwards, nr. Buzzards Bay.
Otter Creek, fort at, VT	Ft. Cassin.
Otter Isl., fort on, SC	St. Helena Sound, Ft. Drayton.
Ouatanon (Ouiatenon, Ouachtanon), Fort, IN	Wabash River, nr. Lafayette.
Overalls Creek, blockhouse on, TN	Near Murfreesboro.
Overton Gen. Hospital, TN	Memphis.
Overton Hill, fortifications on, TN	5 mi. S of Nashville.
Owen, Fort, MT	Bitter Root or St. Marys River.
Owen, Fort, VA	Petersburg.
Owyhee River, Camp, ID	Opp. Ft. Boise.
Ox, Fort, NY	Near source of Allegheny.
Oxford, fort at, MA	
Oxford Park, camp at, PA	3 mi. from Frankford.
Oyster Bay, cantonment at, NY	N shore of Nassau County.
Oyster Island Battery, NY	On Ellis Isl., NY City harbor.
Oyster River, fortified houses on, ME	

Pacific Branch Soldiers' Home, CA   Los Angeles County.
Page, Fort, VA   Near Williamsburg.
Pages Point, battery at, SC
Pagosa Springs, fort at, CO   Ft. Lewis.
Paige, Camp, UT   In San Pete Valley.
Palachocolas, Fort, SC   Savannah River.
Palacios AAF, TX   NW of Palacios.
Paine Field, WA   ESE of Mukilteo.
Palatka Ordnance Depot, FL   Palatka.
Palm Springs AAF, CA   E of Palm Springs.
Palmdale AAF, CA   SSE Lancaster.
Palmer Battery, NY   At Ft. Michie.
Palmer, Camp, NC   Near New Bern.
Palmer, Camp, VA   Near Arlington.
Palmer, Fort, PA   Westmoreland County.
Palmer Island, fort on, MD   Ft. Susquehanna.
Palmer, Lunette, TN   Chattanooga.
Palmetto, Fort, SC   At Stone Inlet.
Palo Alto, Camp, TX   5 mi. below Brownsville.
Panama Park, Camp, FL   Jacksonville.
Panmure, Fort, MS   Natchez.
Parapet, Camp, LA   Near Carrollton.
Pardees Ranch, Post, CA   On old Trinity Trail.
Paris, Fort, NY   At Stone Arabia, Mohawk Valley.
Parish's Fort, WI   Wingville.
Parke, Fort, NC   Roanoke Isl.
Parker, Fort, MT
Parker, Fort, FL   At Cooks Hammock.
Parnamirim Field, Brazil   Natal.
Parole, Camp, MD   Near Annapolis.
Parrott, Battery, VA   At Ft. Monroe.
Parrott, Battery, DC   Potomac River, above Georgetown.
Parrotts Point, battery at, MD   Opp. St. Michaels.
Parsons, Battery, VA   At Curtis' house, near Bermuda Hundred.
Passamaquoddy, defenses of, ME
Pass au Heron, Tower, AL   Mobile Bay.
Passo Cavallo, fortifications at, TX
Patapsco, Fort, MD   Below Baltimore, in Patapsco River.
Patience, Fort, VA   Henrico.
Patrick Henry, Camp, MS   Jackson.
Patrick Henry, Fort, TN   Holston River.
Patterson, Camp, PA   Near Chambersburg.
Patterson Field, OH   NE of Dayton.
Patterson Park Gen. Hospital, MD   Baltimore.
Patterson's Fort, PA   Opp. Mexico, in Tuscarora Valley.
Patterson's Fort, PA   Snyder County.
Pattersonville, fortifications at, LA
Paull's Fort, WV
Paulus Hook, Fort, NJ   Jersey City.
Pavlovski, Fort, AK   Near Kenayan Bay.
Pawnee Agency, Camp at, NE
Payne, Camp, WY   Near Ft. Laramie.
Payne, Fort, AL   Dekalb Co.
Payne, Fort, IL

Pea Patch Island, fort on, DE	Ft. Delaware.
Pearse's Fort, PA	4 mi. from Uniontown.
Pease, Fort, MT	Yellowstone River.
Peat Bay, reservation on, LA	
Pecan Camp, TX	Near Colorado River.
Peck, Battery, NJ	Ft. Hancock.
Peck, Fort, MT	Near mouth of Poplar River.
Pecks Slip, redoubt at, NY	NY City.
Pecontook or Otter Creek, fort at, VT	Ft. Cassin.
Pecos AAF, TX	SW of Pecos.
Peddocks Island, fort on, MA	Ft. Andrews.
Pegan (Pagan) Creek, battery at, VA	
Pegypscot Falls, fort at, ME	
Pelham, fort, MA	
Pelican Spit, reservation at, TX	In Galveston Bay.
Pemaquid, fort at, ME	Ft. Charles.
Pembina, Fort, ND	Red River of the North; ex-Ft. George H. Thomas.
Pemberton, Fort, MS	Near Greenwood.
Pemberton, Fort, VA	New Romney.
Peninsula Island, reservation on, CA	
Penn Fort, PA	Stroudsburg.
Pennacook, fort at, NH	
Pennington, Cantonment, NJ	Trenton.
Penns Cove Reservation, WA	Whidby Isl.
Pennsylvania, Camp, MD	Near Ft. McHenry.
Pennsylvania, Fort, DC	NE of Tennallytown; became Ft. Reno.
Pennsylvania State Soldiers' Home, PA	Erie.
Penobscot Bay/River, fort on, ME	At the narrows of the Penobscot.
Penobscot, Fort, ME	
Penrose Ferry, battery at, PA	
Pensacola Barracks, PA	Pensacola.
Pensacola Battery, FL	Santa Rosa Isl., at Ft. Pickens.
Pensacola Navy Yard, FL	Pensacola.
Pentagoet, Fort, ME	Castine.
Pentagon, The, DC	Washinton.
Penton, Fort, FL	19 mi. from Indian River.
Pepperell, Fort, ME	
Pepperell, Fort, NY	Later site of Ft. Ontario.
Pequod, Fort, KY	2 mi. W of Portersville.
Pequod, Fort, CT	Mystic River.
Peralto Station, NM	Rio Grande, near Albuquerque.
Perdido Bay/River, reservation, FL	
Perine, Camp, NJ	Trenton.
Perkins, Camp, CT	New Haven.
Perrin Field, TX	NW of Sherman.
Perrot, Fort, MN	A/k/a Ft. Secours.
Perry AAF, FL	S of Perry.
Perry AAF, OK	N of Perry.
Perry Battery, KY	Near Covington.
Perry Battery, VA	James River.
Perry, Fort, GA	Marion County.
Peterson Field, CO	E of Colorado Springs.
Petite Coquille, fort at, LA	Ft. Pike.

Pettit Barracks, Philippines	Zamboanga.
Pettus, Camp, MS	Near Enterprise.
Peyton, Fort, FL	Moultrie Creek, near Anastasia Isl.
Peyton, Fort, FL	On Anastasia Isl., near St. Augustine.
Phantom Hill, Fort, TX	Clear Fork of Brazos River.
Phelps, Camp, TX	Rio Grande River, opp. Los Cueras.
Phelps, Fort, TN	Near Missionary Ridge.
Philadelphia Arsenal, PA	Schuylkill Arsenal.
Philadelphia National Cemetery, PA	Philadelphia.
Philip, Fort, LA	Miss. River, Plaquemine Parish (see Ft. St. Philip).
Phil Kearny, Battery, KY	Near Newport (See Kearny, Phil).
Phil Kearny, Fort, WY	Powder River (See Kearny).
Phillips Battery, MS	At Corinth.
Phillips Field, MD	At Aberdeen Proving Ground.
Phillips, Fort, MA	Plum Isl.
Phillips, Fort, PA	Near Williamsburg.
Philpot, Fort, KY	Louisville.
Phoenix, Camp, I.T. (OK)	Became Ft. Towson.
Phoenix, Fort, MA	New Bedford harbor, nr. Fairhaven.
Piatt, Camp, VA	10 mi. above Charleston.
Picatinny Powder Depot, NJ	Dover.
Pickawillany Blockhouses, OH	On Great Miami, Shelby County.
Pickens, Camp, VA	Manassas Junction.
Pickens, Fort, FL	Santa Rosa Isl., Rensacola harbor.
Pickering, Fort, GA	Colerain.
Pickering, Fort, MA	Winter Isl., Salem harbor.
Pickering, Fort, TN	Memphis.
Pickett, Camp, VA	E of Blackstone.
Pickett, Camp, WA	San Juan Isl.
Pierce, Camp, NC	New Bern.
Pierce, Fort. AL	Alabama River, 2 mi. S of Ft. Mimms.
Pierce, Fort, FL	St. Lucie Sound, Brevard Co.
Pierpont, Camp, VA	Ceredo, Wayne Co.
Pierpont, Camp, VA	Prospect Hill, Fairfax Co.
Pierre AAF, SD	Pierre.
Pierre, Fort, SD	Stanley Co.
Piggot's Fort, IL	Near Columbia.
Pig Point, battery at, VA	S of Newport News.
Pike, Battery, LA	At Ft. St. Philip.
Pike, Camp, AR	Conway; became Camp Jos. T. Robinson.
Pike, Fort, LA	Petite Coquille Isl.
Pike, Fort, MO	10 mi. above mouth of Des Moines River.
Pike, Fort, NY	Near Sacket Harbor.
Pike's Cantonment, NY	3 mi. W of Plattsburgh.
Pikes Peak Reservation, CO	Signal Service Reservation.
Pike's Stockade, MN	Falls of Painted Rock, Upper Miss. River.
Pikesville Arsenal, MD	Pikesville.
Pillow, Fort, TN	Miss. River, 40 mi. N of Memphis.
Pilot Butte, Camp, WY	Rock Springs.
Pilot Knob, fort at, MO	Iron County.
Pinal, Camp, AZ	Pinal Mountains; became Infantry Camp.
Pinckney, Camp, GA	Charlton Co.
Pinckney, Castle, SC	Charleston harbor.
Pinecastle AAF, FL	SE of Orlando.

Pinellas AAF, FL	SE of Clearwater.
Pine Ridge Agency, camp at, SD	
Pines, Point of, fort at, SC	Ft. Edisto.
Piney, Fort, WY	Piney Creek, Uintah Co.
Pinney, Fort, AR	Near Helena,
Pinto, Fort, AL	Near Mobile.
Piper Battery, NY	At Ft. Hamilton.
Piper's Fort, PA	In Yellow Creek Valley, Bedford Co.
Piqua, Fort, OH	Miami River, present site of Piqua.
Piscataway, fort at mouth of the, MD	Ft. Washington.
Pitt, Fort, NY	NY City.
Pitt, Fort, PA	Pittsburgh.
Pitt's Fort, TN	Cumberland Gap.
Pittston, Fort, PA	Pittston.
Pittsburg Landing, national cemetery, TN	Shiloh National Cemetery.
Pittsfield, reservation, MA	Berkshire Co.
Pittsford, fort at, VT	Ft. Mott.
Pittstown, Redoubt, PA	Near Wilkes-Barre.
Plattesville, fort at, WI	Grant Co.
Plain, Fort, NY	Montgomery County.
Plank, Fort, NY	Mohawk River, 10 mi. NW of Ft. Plain.
Plaquemine, Fort, LA	Miss. River; became Ft. St. Philip.
Platte, Fort, NE	Jct. of Laramie & Platte Rivers.
Plattsburg Barracks, NY	Plattsburgh.
Pleasant, Fort, FL	Econfinee River.
Pleasant, Fort, WV	S Branch of Potomac.
Ploughed Hill, French redoubt on, MA	Charlestown.
Plum Island, fort on, MA	Merrimac River, Newburyport harbor; Ft. Phillips.
Plum Island, fort on, NY	Ft. Terry, NE of Long Island.
Plum Point, Fort, NY	Hudson River.
Plume, Joseph W., Camp, NY	Buffalo.
Plummer, Camp, NM	Became Ft. Lowell.
Plunkett Battery, MA	At Ft. Warren.
Plymouth, defenses of, NC	
Plymouth, fort at, MA	Ft. Standish.
Plymouth, fort at, PA	Luzerne County.
Pocahontas, Camp, VA	Near Eastville.
Pocahontas, Fort, VA	James River at Wilsons Landing.
Poco, Camp, VA	Kanawha River.
Poinsett, Fort, FL	At Cape Sable.
Point Adams, fort at, OR	Ft. Stevens.
Point, Battery, NC	On Sullivans Isl.
Point Creek, fortifications on, OH	
Point, Fort, CA	At Golden Gate, San Francisco Bay; became Ft. Winfield Scott.
Point, Fort, CT	Fitchs Point, near Norwalk.
Point, Fort, ME	Castine.
Point, Fort, MD	Annapolis.
Point, Fort, MA	Later the site of Ft. Phoenix.
Point, Fort, TX	Became Ft. Jacinto.
Point Hudson Reservation, WA	Near Port Townsend.
Point Isabel, fort at, TX	Ft. Polk.
Point Jerry Reservation, NH	Newcastle.
Point Lobos, fort at, CA	Ft. Miley.

Point Lookout, camp at, MD	Camp Hoffman.
Point Lorna Reservation, CA	Lorna Point.
Point of Rocks, battery, NY	Near Harlem area, NY City.
Point Patience, fort on, MD	Patuxent River.
Point Peter, battery at, GA	St. Marys River.
Point Pleasant, battery at, MO	Miss. River, 12 mi. below New Madrid.
Point Roberts Reservation, WA	On Puget Sound.
Point San Jose, fort at, CA	Became Ft. Mason.
Point Wilson Reservation, WA	Entr. to Admiralty Inlet.
Poland, Camp, TN	Knoxville.
Polk, Camp, ID	
Polk, Camp, TN	On Island #10.
Polk, Fort, LA	Lake Charles.
Polk, Fort, TX	At Point Isabel, Gulf of Mexico.
Pollock AAF, LA	N of Alexandria.
Pompey, old fortifications at, NY	
Pompton Plains, camp at, NJ	
Ponca (Ponka), Fort, SD	Missouri River, at Ponca Agency.
Poncas Island, Camp, NE	Missouri River, nr. mouth of Ponca Creek.
Pond Creek, Camp, KS	Became Ft. Wallace.
Pond, Fort, MO	St. Charles Co., near Wentzville.
Pond Hill, Battery, NC	Near Ft. Fisher.
Ponchartrain, Fort, MI	Detroit.
Pontoosack, Fort, MA	Housatonic River.
Pool's Fort, CA	Kings River, Fresno Co.
Pooplopens Kill, Fort, Fort, NY	In the Highlands.
Pope Field, NC	At Ft. Bragg.
Popham, Fort, ME	On Hunnewells Point, mouth of Kennebec River.
Poplar Grove National Cemetery, VA	Near Petersburg.
Poplar River, Camp, MT	Near Poplar Creek Agency.
Poposquash Neck, battery at, RI	Narragansett Bay.
Portage des Sieux, Fort, MO	Miss. River, nr. Bellefontaine.
Portage, Fort, OH	Portage River, Wood Co.
Port Angeles AAF, WA	Port Angeles.
Port Angeles & Ediz Hook Reservation, WA	Clallam County.
Porter, Battery, VA	At Ft. Hunt.
Porter, Camp, UT	In San Pete Valley.
Porter, Fort, ME	Castine.
Porter, Fort, NY	Buffalo.
Porterville AAF, CA	SW of Porterville.
Port Hudson, fortifications at, LA	
Port Hudson National Cemetery, LA	Port Hudson.
Port Royal Roads, forts at, SC	
Portsmouth, battery at, NC	Portsmouth.
Portuguese Air Base #4, Azores	Terceira Isl.; became Lajes Field.
Port Valdez, fort at, AK	Ft. Liscum.
Possum Nose, battery at, VA	Potomac River, below Cockpit Point.
Post Field, OK	At Ft. Sill.
Potato Battery, MD	At Havre de Grace.
Potomac Creek, batteries on, VA	On Lower Potomac.
Potter's Fort, PA	Center County.

Potter, Battery, NJ	At Ft. Hancock.
Potter, Camp, VA	Near Bermuda Hundred.
Pounds Field, TX	W of Tyler.
Poverty Point, fort at, LA	Ft. Mississippi.
Powder Point, battery on, MO	At St. Louis.
Powder River, fort on, WY	Ft. Phil Kearny.
Powell, Fort, AL	Heron Isl., Mobile Bay.
Powell, Fort, MS	Near Corinth.
Powell, Fort, WV	
Powers, Camp, ME	Augusta.
Powhatan, Fort, VA	James River, nr. Little Brandon.
Powles Hook, fort at, NJ	Same as Paulus Hook.
Pownall, Fort, ME	Castine.
Prairie du Chien, fort at, WI	Ft. Crawford.
Prairie Island, stockade on, MN	Near Lake Pepin.
Prairieville Aux. AAF, AR	W of Almyra.
Pratt AAF, KS	N of Pratt.
Preble, Fort, ME	Spring Point, Portland Harbor.
Prentiss, Camp, CA	Near San Bernardino.
Prentiss, Fort, IL	Cairo.
Prescott Barracks, AZ	Became Whipple Barracks.
Prescott, Camp, CA	Near Darnestown.
Prescott, Fort, VA	Near Petersburg.
Presentation, Fort, VA	Ogdensburg.
Presidio of Monterey, CA	Monterey.
Presidio of San Diego, CA	San Diego.
Presidio of San Francisco, CA	San Francisco.
Presidio of Santa Barbara, CA	Santa Barbara.
Presque Isle AAF, ME	Presque Isle.
Presque Isle, fort at, ME	Ft. Erie.
Preston, Fort, FL	Apalachicola River.
Price, Camp, GA	Macon.
Price, Camp, I.T. (OK)	Near Arkansas City.
Pricket's Fort, WV	Monongahela River, 12 mi. above Morgantown.
Prince Charles, Redoubt, NY	On Valentines Hill, SE part of NY State.
Prince, Fort, NY	At Kingsbridge, Bronx County.
Prince George, Fort, GA	
Prince George, Fort, SC	Savannah River, 300 from Charleston.
Prince Maurice, Fort, NY	Hudson River.
Prince William, Fort, ME	Pemaquid.
Pringle, Battery, SC	James Island.
Prior, Camp, GA	Near Macon.
Proctors Landing, or Proctorsville Tower, LA	
Prospect Hill, work on, MA	At The Citadel, Charlestown.
Protection Island Reservation, CA	Entr. to Port Discovery.
Providence, fort at, RI	On College Hill.
Province Island, fortifications on, PA	Near Ft. Mifflin.
Provincetown, battery at, MA	Long Point Battery.
Prudhomme, Fort, IL	180 mi. above mouth of Illinois River.
Prudhomme. Fort, TN	Near Memphis.
Pruyn Battery, VA	Near Richmond.
Pueblo AAF, CO	ENE of Pueblo.

Pueblo, fort at, CO	
Pueblo, Fort, AR	Ft. Reynolds.
Puget Sound Narrows Reservation, WA	Arkansas River, above Ft. Bent.
Pulaski, Fort, GA	
Puleston, Camp, PA	Cockspur Isl., Savannah harbor.
Pungoteague Inlet, battery at, VA	Near Philadelphia.
Punta Gorda AAF, FL	Chesapeake Bay.
Puntarassa, fort at, FL	ESE of Punta Gorda.
Purviance, Battery, SC	Ft. Dulany.
Put-in-Bay, blockhouse/battery at, OH	On Morris Isl.
Putnam, Camp, OH	
Putnam, Fort, NY	
Putnam, Fort, SC	On Mt. Independence, West Point.
Putnam Redoubt, TN	Cummings Point, Charleston harbor.
Putney, Fort, VT	Chattanooga.
Pyote AAF, TX	Connecticut River, Windham Co.
	SW of Monahans.

Quakers Hill, post on, RI	
Quantico River, battery near, VA	
Quarantine, Fort, NC	Cape Fear River, nr. Ft. Fisher.
Quatre Bayou Pass Reservation, LA	
Queen Anne's Fort, RI	Goat Isl., subsite Ft. Walcott.
Quincy National Cemetery, NJ	Quincy.
Quintons Bridge, Breastworks, NJ	5 mi. SE of Salem.
Quitman, Fort, TX	On the Rio Grande, 70 mi. below El Paso.

Racoon, Fort, IA — Became Ft. Des Moines.
Radziminski, Camp, I.T. OK) — On Otter Creek.
Rains. Camp, SD — At Spotted Tail Agency.
Rains, Colonel, Camp, KY — Cumberland Gap.
Raleigh-Durham AAF, NC — NW of Raleigh-Durham.
Raleigh National Cemetery, NC — Raleigh.
Ralston, Fort, PA — Northampton Co., a/k/a Brown's Fort.
Ramey Field, PR —
Rampart, Camp, AK — Rampart City.
Ramsay, Battery, ME — At Ft. McKinley.
Ramsay, Battery, SC — James Island.
Ramsay, Fort, VA — Near Washington, DC.
Ramsey, Camp, MN — Near St. Paul.
Ramsours Mill, camp near, NC — Lincoln County.
Rancho del Chino, Post, CA — 30 mi. SE of Los Angeles.
Rancho de Jurupa, Post, CA — Santa Ana River.
Randall, Camp, WI — Madison.
Randall, Fort, SD — Missouri River, Gegory Co., near Nebraska border.

Randolph, Camp, OR — Three-Mile Creek, nr. Ft. Dallas.
Randolph, Field, TX — Universal City.
Randolph, Fort, Panama — Canal Zone.
Randolph, Fort, TN — Randolph.
Randolph, Fort, WV — Mouth of Great Kanawha.
Ranger, Fort, VT —
Rankin, Camp, CO — Julesburg; became Ft. Sedgwick.
Rankin's Fort, AL — Near Mobile River.
Ransom, Battery, LA — At Ft. Jackson.
Ransom, Battery, MS — Vicksburg.
Ransom, Fort, ND — Cheyenne River, Ransom Co.
Rapid, Camp, SD — Rapid City.
Rapid City Army Air Base, SD — NE of Rapid City.
Rapp, Camp, DC — At Kendall Green, Washington.
Rawdon, Field, KS — E of Wichita.
Rawlins, Camp, AZ — In Williamsons Valley, 27 mi. NW of Prescott.

Rawlins, Fort, MS — Vicksburg.
Rawlins, Fort, UT — Near Provo.
Raystown, Fort, PA — On Raystown Branch.
Read, Battery, DE — At Fort DuPont.
Read, Fort, Trinidad — Cumuto.
Reading AAF, PA — N of Reading.
Reading, Fort, CA — Shasta County.
Reading, Fort, PA — W bank of Delaware River.
Record Gen. Hospital, DC — Washington.
Recovery, Fort, OH — Mercer County.
Redan, Fort, TN — Above Island #10.
Red Bank, Redoubt, NJ — Near Ft. Mifflin.
Redding AAF, CA — SE of Redding.
Red, Fort, AL — Near Spanish Fort.
Red Hook, battery at, NY — Brooklyn.
Redmond AAF, OR — SE of Redmond.
Red Redoubt, VA — At Yorktown.
Red River, fort on, AR —

Red Rock Reservation, CA	Molate Isl., San Francisco harbor.
Redstone Arsenal, AL	Huntsville.
Redstone, Fort, PA	Later the site of Brownsville.
Red Willow, Camp, NE	Near Republican River, 1 mi. above mouth of Red Willow Creek.
Reed, Camp, ID	Snake River.
Reed, Camp, VA	Near Alexandria.
Reed, Fort, FL	Nr. Lake Monroe, Orange Co.
Reed, Fort, NY	Schoharie Co.
Reeves Point, fortifications on, NC	Near Wilmington.
Rehoboth, fortifications at, MA	
Reid, Fort, PA	Lock Haven.
Reilly, Battery, RI	At Ft. Adams.
Reilly, Camp, PA	Williamsport.
Reiter, Fort, AR	Near Helena.
Release, Camp, MN	Near mouth of Chippewa River.
Reliance, Fort, AK	Yukon River.
Relief, Camp, DC	Washington.
Relief, Camp, TX	Eagle Springs, Cimbria River.
Reme Snyder's Blockhouse, NY	NE of Little Falls.
Remount Camp, MD	In Pleasant Valley.
Remount, Camp, VA	Alexandria.
Reno AAF, NV	Reno.
Reno, Camp, AZ	In Tonto Valley.
Reno, Camp, NC	New Bern.
Reno, Camp, WI	Milwaukee.
Reno, Cantonment, WY	Became Ft. McKinney.
Reno, Fort, DC	NE of Tennallytown; ex-Ft. Pennsylvania.
Reno, Fort, NC	Roanoke Isl.
Reno, Fort, OK	N fork of Canadian River, 2 mi. SW of Cheyenne & Arapaho Agency.
Reno, Fort, VA	Near Portsmouth.
Reno, Fort, WY (1st)	Powder River; ex-Ft. Connor.
Reno, Fort, WY (2nd)	Powder River; 3 mi. N of old Ft. Reno.
Rensselaer, Fort, NY	At Canajoharie, in Mohawk Valley.
Republic, Fort, VA	S fork of the Shenandoah.
Resaca, fortifications at, GA	
Resurrection, Fort, AK	On SE coast.
Return, Camp, PA	Near Harrisburg.
Revere, Fort, MA	Hull.
Reviers, Fort, AL	Betweenn Alabama & Tombigbee Rivers.
Reynolds, Battery, NJ	At Ft. Hancock.
Reynolds, Battery, SC	Morris Island.
Reynolds, Camp, CA	Angel Isl.; became Ft. McDowell.
Reynolds, Camp, MT	S bank of Sun River; became Ft. Shaw.
Reynolds, Camp, PA	Pittsburgh.
Reynolds, Fort, CO	Arkansas River.
Reynolds, Fort, PA	Washington, Co.
Reynolds, Fort, VA	3 mi. NW of Alexandria.
Reynolds, Joe, Camp, IN	Near Indianapolis.
Rhode Island, Fort, RI	
Rhode Island State Soldier's Home, RI	Bristol.
Rice AAF, CA	SE of Rice.
Rice, Camp, TX	Became Ft. Hancock.

Rice, Fort, ND	Missouri River, Morton Co.
Rice, Fort, PA	Near Washingtonville.
Rice, Fort, VA	Near Petersburg.
Rice's Fort, MA	Charleroi.
Rice's Fort, WV	Buffalo Creek, 14 mi. from Ohio River.
Richards, Fort, WV	On the Monongahela.
Richardson, Fort, AK	Near Anchorage, at Elmendorf Field.
Richardson, Fort, MS	Near Corinth.
Richardson, Fort, TX	Lost Creek, nr. Jacksboro.
Richardson, Fort, VA	About 3 mi. from Washington, DC.
Richmond Arsenal, VA	Near Richmond.
Richmond, Battery, NY	At. Ft. Wadsworth.
Richmond, Fort, ME	W bank of the Kennebec, opp. Swan Isl.
Richmond, Fort, NY	Staten Isl.; became Ft. Wadsworth.
Richmond, Fort, VA	On battleground of Fair Oaks.
Richmond National Cemetery, VA	Richmond.
Rickets, Fort, WV	
Ricketts, Camp, TX	Edinburg, on Rio Grande.
Ricketts, Fort, DC	E of the Eastern Branch.
Ricketts, Fort, WV	
Rickey, Fort, NY	
Riddle's Fort, KY	At forks of the Licking.
Riddle's Fort, WV	Lost River.
Ridgely, Battery, LA	At Ft. St. Philip.
Ridgely, Fort, MN	Nicollet Co., on Minnesota River.
Riffle, Fort, PA	Fayette County.
Rigolets, fort at, LA	Nr. Lake Pontchartrain; Ft. Pike.
Rikers Island, draft depot at, NY	East River, NY City.
Riley, Camp, CA	12 mi. from San Diego.
Riley, Fort, KS	Nr. Junction City; ex-Camp Centre.
Riley, Fort, TN	Near Nashville.
Riley, Fort, TX	Las Moras Creek; became Ft. Clark.
Ringgold, Fort, TX	Near Rio Grande City.
Rio Gila Depot, NM	S of Mofollon Mountains.
Rio Verde Reservation, AZ	Indian Reservation.
Ripley, Battery, MA	At Ft. Revere.
Ripley, Camp, MN	SW of Brainerd; ex-Ft. Ripley.
Ripley, Camp, Aux. Field, MN	SW of Brainerd.
Ripley, Fort, MN	Crow Wing Co.; ex-Ft. Gaines; became Camp Ripley.
Ripley, Fort, MD	2 mi. above Chain Bridge, DC; became Redoubt Cross.
Ripley, Fort, SC	In Charleston harbor.
Rip Raps, fort on the, VA	Ft. Wood.
Ritchie, Battery, DE	At Ft. Dupont.
Ritchie, Fort, MD	Near Waynesboro, PA.
Ritner, Fort, IN	Lawrence County.
Roach, Fort, KS	Southern border of Neosho Co.
Roanoke, fort at, NC	
Roanoke Island, forts on, NC	Forts Barton, Blanchard, Burnside, Defiance, Ellis, Forrest, Foster, Huger, Lane, Montiel, Parke, Reno, Russell & Sullivan.
Roberdeau, Fort, PA	In Sinking Valley, a/k/a Lead Mine Fort.
Roberts, Camp, CA	Monterey Peninsula.

Roberts Field, Liberia	Monrovia.
Roberts Point Reservation, WA	See Point Roberts.
Robinette, Fort, MS	Near Corinth.
Robins Field, GA	NE of Wellston.
Robinson, Battery, VA	At Ft. Hunt.
Robinson, Camp, AR	Near Little Rock.
Robinson, Fort, NE	White River, at the Red Cloud Agency.
Robinsons Point, battery at, ME	St. Georges River.
Rochambeau Field, French Guiana	Cayenne.
Rock, Fort, CT	Became Ft. Hale.
Rockfort, Fort, IL	Illinois River, Lasalle Co.
Rock Island Armory & Arsenal, IL	Roch Island.
Rock Island National Cemetery, IL	Rock Island.
Rockland Field, ME	ESE of Rockland.
Rock Point, fort at, MD	Ft. Smallwood.
Rock Springs, camp at, WY	Camp Pilot Butte.
Rockwell Field, CA	Coronado.
Rodger's Bastion, MD	Baltimore.
Rodgers, Battery, VA	Alexandria.
Rodgers, Camp, FL	Ybor City.
Rodman, Fort, MA	Clarks Point, near New Bedford.
Rodman, Fort, VA	Near Portsmouth.
Rodmans Point, battery at, NC	Near Washington.
Rodney, Battery, DE	At Ft. Dupont.
Rogue River, Camp, OR	Mouth of Rogue River.
Roller's Fort, PA	In Sinking Valley.
Rome Air Depot, NY	Rome.
Rome Arsenal, NY	Rome.
Romulus AAF, MI	SW of Detroit.
Roney's Fort, PA	Finley Township, Washington Co.
Roosevelt Field, NY	Mineola, Nassau County.
Root, Camp, KS	At Ft. Riley.
Rosa, Fort, FL	W end of Santa Rosa Isl., SE Pensacola.
Rosalie, Fort, MS	Natchez.
Rosecrans Battery, VA	Near Suffolk.
Rosecrans, Camp, IL	Near Quincy.
Rosecrans Field, MO	W of Springfield.
Rosecrans, Fort, CA	San Diego.
Rosedew, Fort, GA	Vernon River.
Rose Island, fort on. RI	Ft. Hamilton.
Ross, Fort, CA	Sonoma Co., on coast, 40 mi. N of Bodega Bay.
Ross, Fort, TN	Tennessee River.
Rossell, Battery, DC	Near Tennallytown.
Roswell AAF, NM	S of Roswell.
Roubideau's Fort, CO	
Round Island Reservation, MS	
Rouses Point, fort at, NY	Ft. Montgomery.
Rowan, Fort, NC	Near New Bern.
Rowley, Cantonment, MD	Potomac River, nr. the Great Falls.
Roxbury Falls, Fort, MA	Near Boston.
Royal Blockhouse, NY	E end of Oneida Lake.
Royal Blockhouse, NY	Wood Creek.
Royal, Fort, ME	Portland; see Fort Loyal.
Royal, Fort, VA	Pamunkey River.

Royalhannon, Fort, PA	See Loyal Hanna & Ligonier.
Ruby, Fort, NV	In Ruby Valley.
Rucker, Camp, VA	Near Falls Church.
Rucker, Fort, AL	Near Ozark.
Rucker, J.A., Camp, AZ	In White River Canyon; ex-Camp Supply.
Ruff, Camp, NJ	Camden.
Ruff, Camp, PA	Philadelphia.
Rugeleys Mills, Camp at, SC	
Ruger, Fort, HI	
Ruggles, Camp, NE	N fork of Loup River, 2 mi. from Ft. Hartsuff.
Ruhlen, Camp, SD	Became Ft. Meade.
Runyon, Fort, VA	Near the Long Bridge, opp. Washington.
Rupert, Fort, WA	Vancouver Island.
Russell, Battery, NC	Roanoke Isl.
Russell, Camp, I.T. (OK)	Near Ft. Reno.
Russell, Camp, OR	Near Salem.
Russell, D.A., Fort, WY	3 mi. from Cheyenne.
Russell, Dan, Camp, NC	Raleigh.
Russell, Fort, FL	Orange Lake Creek, 6 mi. from Tampa.
Russell, Fort, TN	Loudon.
Russell, Fort, IL	Near Edwardsville.
Russel's Garrison, ME	Dartmouth.
Rutgers Hill, Battery, NY	NY City.
Rutland, fortifications at, VT	
Rudledge, Battery, SC	
Ryan, Battery, SC	James Island.
Ryerson's Fort, PA	Greene County.

A Union soldier strikes a dashing pose during the Civil War.

Sabine, Fort, LA	Sabine Lake, 3 mi. below Sabine City.
Sabine, Fort, TX	In Sabine Pass, Jefferson Co.
Sacandaga, blockhouse at, NY	Schoharie County.
Sac and Fox Agency, IA	
Saco, Fort, ME	Saco River, near the falls.
Sacket Camp, VA	Near Alexandria.
Sacket Harbor, post at, NY	Madison Barracks.
Sackville, Fort, IN	Vincennes.
Sacramento Air Depot, CA	Sacramento.
Sacramento, fort at, CA	Sutters Fort.
Sadler, Camp, NV	Carson City.
Saguina (Saginaw) Bay, fort at, MI	On Lake Huron.
St. Andrews Sound, fort at, GA	Cumberland Isl.
St. Anne, Fort, NY	Isle La Motte, Lk. Champlain; a/k/a Ft. La Motte.
St. Anthony, Fort, MN	Became Ft. Snelling.
St. Asaphs, Fort, KY	A/k/a Logan's Fort.
St. Augustine, fort at, FL	Became Ft. Marion.
St. Augustine National Cemetery, FL	St. Augustine.
St. Bernard, Fort, FL	Pensacola.
St. Bernard Bay, fort on, TX	
St. Carlos, Fort, FL	Near Fernandina.
St. Catherines Sound, fortifications on, GA	
St. Charles, Battery, AR	Near White River.
St. Charles (or San Carlos), Fort, FL	Became Ft. Barrancas.
St. Charles, Fort, LA	New Orleans.
St. Charles, Fort, ME	Pemaquid.
St. Charles, Fort, MO	St. Louis.
St. Clair, Fort, OH	On St. Clair River, nr. Eaton.
St. Clair Morton, Fort, KY	Nr. Louisville; see Morton, St. Clair.
St. Croix Island, Fort, ME	Schoodic River.
St. Dionysius, Redoubt, AK	At Ft. Wrangell.
St. Elizabeth Gen. Hospital, DC	Washington.
St. Ferdinand, Fort, LA	New Orleans.
St. Fernando, Fort, TN	About 3 mi. from Memphis.
St. Francis Barracks, FL	St. Augustine.
St. Francis de Pupa, Fort, FL	St. Johns River.
St. Francis, Fort, AR	Mouth of St. Francis River.
St. Frederic, Fort, NC	New Orleans.
St. George, Fort, FL	Amelia Island.
St. George, Fort, ME	Philippsburg.
St. George, Fort, ME	Thomaston.
St. George, Fort, NY	Smiths Point, Mastic, Suffolk Co.
St. George, Fort, RI	
St. Georges Bay/River, fort on, ME	
St. Georges Sound Reservation, FL	
St. Helena Sound, fort on, SC	Ft. Fremont.
St. Ingoes, Fort, MD	Near St. Marys.
St. James Gen. Hospital, LA	New Orleans.
St. John, Camp, VA	Fairfax County.
St. John, Fort, LA	Lake Pontchartrain, nr. New Orleans.
St. John, Fort, NY	

St. Johns Bluff, battery at, FL	Mouth of St. Johns River.
St. Johns Hill, battery at, KY	Near Newport.
St. John the Baptist, Fort, NM	On the Rio del Norte.
St. John the Baptist, Fort, TX	W bank of the Rio Bravo.
St. Joseph, Fort, IL	Nr. head of the Illinois River.
St. Joseph, Fort, LA	New Orleans.
St. Joseph, Fort, MI	Lake Huron; later the site of Ft. Gratiot.
St. Josephs, Fort, FL	On St. Josephs Bay.
St. Joseph's Gen Hospital, NY	NY City.
St. Josephs River, fort at, MI	At mouth of river.
St. Leon, Fort, LA	15 mi. below New Orleans.
St. Louis Barracks, MO	St. Louis.
St. Louis Clothing Depot, MO	St. Louis.
St. Louis de Carloretto, Fort, TX	Natchitoches River.
St. Louis de la Mobile, Fort, AL	On Mobile Bay.
St. Louis, Fort, IL	Rockford.
St. Louis, Fort, LA	New Orleans.
St. Louis, Fort, MS	Bay of Biloxi.
St. Louis, Fort, TX	Near Matagorda Bay.
St. Louis Powder Depot, MO	At Jefferson Barracks.
St. Marks, Fort, FL	St. Marks River.
St. Marks, Fort, OH	Mercer County.
St. Mary de Apalachee, Fort, FL	Mouth of Ocklockonnee River.
St. Marys, fort at, MD	Potomac River; Ft. St. Ingoes.
St. Marys, Fort, OH	St. Marys.
St. Marys, Fort, MI	On St. Marys Strait.
St. Marys Gen. Hospital, NY	Rochester.
St. Michael, Fort, AK	St. Michaels Isl.
St. Michael, Fort, FL	Pensacola.
St. Michaels, Redoubt, AK	St. Michaels Isl.
St. Nicholas, Fort, AK	Became Ft. Kenay.
St. Paul Island, reservation/post on, AK	
St. Peter, Fort, MS	Yazoo River.
St. Philip, Fort, AL	Mobile River, 20 mi. above Mobile.
St. Philip, Fort, LA	Miss. River, 65 mi. below New Orleans.
St. Philip, Fort, NC	At Old Brunswick, Cape Fear River.
St. Rose, Fort/Battery, FL	Opp. Ft. Barrancas.
St. Simeons, Fort, AK	Near Cape Elias.
St. Simons, Fort, GA	St. Simons Isl.
St. Stephens, Fort, AL	Tombigbee River, 142 mi. SW Montgomery.
St. Tommany (Tammany), Fort, GA	Mouth of St. Marys River.
St. Vincent, Fort, IN	Vincennes.
St. Vincent Island, battery on, FL	
St. Vrains, Fort, CO	S fork Platte River.
Saffold, Battery, CA	At the Presidio.
Salem, fort near, NJ	Ft. Mott.
Salinas AAF, CA	E of Salinas.
Salisbury National Cemetery, NC	Salisbury.
Salisbury Point, fort at, MA	Ft. Nichols.
Sallie Olden, Camp, TN	Near Triune.
Salonga, Fort, NY	NW Suffolk Co.
Salmon Falls, fort at, NH	
Salt Lake, camp at, TX	85 mi. NW of Ft. Brown.
Salt Meadow, fort at, NY	

Salubrity, Camp, LA	3 mi. from Natchitoches.
Salvador, Fort, SC	
Sam Houston, Fort, TX	San Antonio.
Sampson, Camp, NY	Kingston.
Sampson, Fort, VA	Near Petersburg.
Sams Point, fort on, SC	Mouth of Coosa River.
San Angelo AAF, TX	SW of San Angelo.
San Antonio Arsenal, TX	San Antonio.
San Antonio de Valere, Fort, TX	About 1 mi. from San Antonio.
San Antonio National Cemetery, TX	San Antonio.
San Bernardino AAF, CA	SE of San Bernardino.
San Bernardino, Camp, CA	On Dead Man's Island.
San Carlos Indian Reservation, AZ	
San Carlos, Battery, CA	Monterey.
San Carlos de Barrancas, Fort, FL	Ft. Barrancas.
San Diego Barracks, CA	San Diego.
San Diego, fort at, CA	Ft. Rosecrans.
San Diego, Fort, FL	Near St. Augustine.
Sand Island Reservation, OR	Near entr. of Columbia River.
San Felipe, Camp, CA	On San Felipe Creek.
San Francisco National Cemetery, CA	At the Presidio.
San Jacinto, Fort, TX	Near Galveston.
San Joaquin, Fort, CA	Entr. to San Francisco Bay; later the site of Ft. Winfield Scott.
San Jose Aux. Field, CA	E of San Jose.
San Jose Field, Philippines	Mindoro
San Jose Point, Fort, CA	On San Francisco Bay; later the site of Ft. Mason.
San Juan de Pinos, Fort, FL	At St. Augustine.
San Juan Island, camp on, WA	Camps Reynolds & Pickett.
San Luis Obispo, Camp, CA	NW of San Luis Obispo.
San Marco Castle, FL	At Ft. Marion, St. Augustine.
San Marco, Fort, FL	St, Marks.
San Marcos AAF, TX	W of San Marcos.
San Marcos de Apalachee, Fort, FL	Same as St, Marks.
San Marcos, Fort, FL	A/k/a Castle San Marco & Ft. Marion.
San Mateo (Matheo), Castle, FL	Same as Ft. Caroline.
San Michael, Castle, FL	St. Augustine.
San Miguel, Camp, CA	In Tulare Valley.
San Nicolas Island Field, CA	San Nicolas Isl.
San Pablo Bay Reservation, CA	
San Pedro Reservation, CA	
Sand Bar Ferry, fort at, SC	Ft. Moore.
Sanders, Fort, TN	Near Knoxville.
Sanders, Fort, WY	3 mi. from Laramie; ex-Ft. John Buford.
Sanderson, Fort, FL	Near Gareys Ferry, E Florida.
Sandford, Fort, IA	Des Moines River, 65 mi. W of Ft. Madison.
Sandhocken, Fort, DE	See Ft. Casimir.
Sand Island Reservation, OR	Entr. to Columbia River.
Sandusky, fort at, OH	Ft. Stephenson.
Sandy Creek, old fort on, NY	Near Lake Ontario.
Sandy Hook, fort at, NJ	Ft. Hancock.
Sanger, Camp, KY	Lexington.
Santa Barbara, camp at, CA	Santa Barbara.
Santa Barbara, Fort, TX	

Santa Barbara, Presidio of, CA	Santa Barbara.
Santa Fe AAF, NM	Santa Fe.
Santa Fe, fort at, NM	Ft. Marcy.
Santa Fe National Cemetery, NM	Santa Fe.
Santa Isabel, Camp, CA	60 mi. E of San Diego.
Santa Maria AAF, CA	NNW of Orcutt.
Santa Maria de Loreto de la Bahia del Espirita Santo, Fort, TX	
	A/k/a Ft. Texas.
Santa Rosa AAF, CA	NW of Fulton.
Santa Rosa Island, fort on, FL	Ft. Pickens.
Santiago, Fort. Philippines	Luzon.
Sarasota AAF, FL	N of Sarasota.
Sarasto, Fort, NY	Hudson River; a/k/a Ft. George.
Saratoga, Fort, DC	Near Washington.
Saratoga, Fort, NY	Saratoga.
Sarpy, Fort, MT	Yellowstone River; Gallatin Co.
Sassafras Point, battery at, RI	Narragansett Bay.
Satartia, fort at, MS	Yazoo River.
Sater, Battery, VA	At Ft. Hunt.
Satterlee Gen. Hospital, PA	Philadelphia.
Sault Ste. Marie, fort at, MI	Ft. Brady.
Saunders, Alvin, Camp, NE	Lincoln.
Saunders, Fort, KS	4 mi. SE of Clinton.
Saunders, Fort, KY	Louisville.
Savannah, Fort, GA	Savannah.
Savannah, Fort, WV	A/k/a Camp Union.
Sawyer, Battery, VA	At Crow Nest.
Saybrook, Fort, CT	On Tomb Hill, mouth of Conn. River.
Scammell, Fort, ME	House Island, Portland harbor,
Scarborough, Fort, ME	At Black Point.
Schafer, Camp, TN	Near Murfreesboro.
Schenck, Battery, AL	At Ft. Morgan.
Schenectady, Fort, NY	Near Schenectady.
Schlosser, Fort, NY	Niagara River, ½-mi. W of mouth of Gill Creek.
Schofield Barracks, HI	25 mi. N of Honolulu.
Schofield, Camp, I.T. (OK)	7 mi. SE of Arkansas City.
Schofield, Camp, VA	Near Lynchburg.
Schofield, Camp, MA	Lynnfield.
Schuyler, Fort, NY (#2)	Throgs Neck, Bronx.
Schuyler. Fort. NY (#1)	Rome.
Schwartz, Fort, PA	Near Milton.
Scott, Battery, LA	At Ft. St. Philip.
Scott, Battery, GA	Tybee Isl.,
Scott, Camp, MA	Worcester.
Scott, Camp, PA	Near York.
Scott, Camp, UT	On Blacks Fork of Green River.
Scott, Camp, VA	Near Alexandria.
Scott, Camp, VA	At Carnifex Ferry.
Scott, Camp, VA	Near Cross Lake.
Scott Field, IL	Belleville.
Scott, Fort, FL	Chattahoochee River, NE of Sneads.
Scott, Fort, GA	Near mouth of Flint River.

Scott, Fort, GA	Near mouth of Flint River.
Scott, Fort, KS	Bourbon County.
Scott, Fort, NY	Plattsburgh.
Scott, Fort, OH	Near mouth of Scioto River.
Scott. Fort, VA	At four Mile Creek.
Scott, Fort National Cemetery, KS	Bourbon County.
Scott, M.J., Camp, TX	Near Rio Grande, 28 mi. NW of Eagle Pass.
Scott, Martin, Battery, DC	Near Chain Bridge.
Scottsbluff AAF, NE	E of Scottsbluff.
Scotts Lake, Fort on, SC	Ft. Watson.
Scott, Winfield, Camp, DC	Franklin Square.
Scott, Winfield, Camp, NM	Gallinas River.
Scott, Winfield, Camp, NV	In Paradise Valley.
Scott, Winfield, Fort, CA	At the Presidio of San Francisco.
Scott, Winfield, Fort, VA	Near Yorktown.
Screven, Fort, GA	Tybee Island.
Scribner AAF, NE	SSE of Scribner.
Sea Brook, battery at, SC	
Searle, Fort, FL	Near Picolata.
Seattle Port of Embarkation, WA	Seattle.
Seawell Field, Barbados	Bridgetown.
Secession, Camp, KY	Ellicotts Mills, near Cairo.
Secessionville, battery near, SC	Jones Island.
Seclusion, Camp, NE	Near mouth of Little Missouri.
Sedalia AAF, MO	2 mi. S of Knob Noster.
Sedgwick, Barracks, DC	Washington.
Sedgwick Battery, RI	At Ft. Greble.
Sedgwick, Fort, CO	S Fork of Platte River; ex-Camp Rankin.
Sedgwick. Fort. VA	Petersburg; a/k/a Ft. Hell.
Sedgwick Gen. Hospital, KY	Louisville.
Sedgwick Gen. Hospital, LA	Greenville.
Selden, Fort, LA	
Selden, Fort, NM	9 mi. from Dona Ana.
Selfridge Field, MI	Mt. Clemens.
Selfield AAF, AL	NE of Selma.
Selman Field, LA	NE of Monroe.
Seminary, Camp, VA	Near Alexandria.
Seminary Gen. Hospital, DC	Georgetown.
Seminary Gen. Hospital, KY	Covington.
Seminary Gen. Hospital, OH	Columbus.
Seminole Battery, FL	Key West.
Semmes Battery, VA	James River.
Seneca Army Depot, NY	Romulus.
Seneca, Old Fort, OH	Seneca Co., Sandusky River, 9 mi. N of Tiffin.
Sequoia National Park, reservation/camp at, CA	
Seraf, Fort, AL	Mobile Point.
Seven, Number, Battery, KY	Near Isl. #10.
Seven-Mile Reach Battery, VA	Appomattox River.
Seven Pines National Cemetery, VA	Henrico County.
Severn, Fort, MD	Annapolis; became US Naval Academy.
Sevier, Camp, SC	Greenville.
Sewall, Fort, MA	Marblehead.
Sewalls Point, fort at, VA	Ft. Boushs Bluff.

Seward, Fort, CA	Eel River, 65 mi. SE of Humboldt.
Seward, Fort, ND	Nr. headwaters of James River; ex-Ft. Cross.
Seward, Fort, SC	On Bay Point.
Seybert, Fort, WV	Pendleton Co., on Moorefield River.
Seymour, Battery, SC	Charleston harbor,
Seymour Johnson Field, NC	SE of Goldsboro.
Shackelford, Fort, FL	In Big Cypress Swamp.
Shafter, Fort, HI	Honolulu.
Shallowbug Bay, Fort, NC	Roanoke Island.
Shamokin, fort at, PA	
Shanesville, fort at, OH	
Shanks, Camp, IN	Indianapolis.
Shannon, Fort, FL	Palatka,.
Shattucks, Fort, NH	Hinsdale.
Shaver's Summit Field, CA	W of Desert Center.
Shaw Field, SC	NW of Sumter.
Shaw, Fort, MT	Sun River, 83 mi. N of Helena; ex-Camp Reynolds.
Shaw, Fort, NC	Wilmington.
Shaw, Fort, SC	Morris Island.
Shaw Island Reservation, WA	In the Haro Archipelago.
Shawnee, Fort, PA	Near Plymouth.
Shawnee, Fort, WV	Mouth of Kanawha River.
Shaws Neck, fort at, CT	New London.
Shaws Point, battery at, ME	
Sheepscot Bay, fort at, ME	Ft. Wiscasset.
Sheffield, fort at, MA	
Shelby, Camp, MS	Hattiesburg.
Shelby, Fort, IL	On later site of Rock Isl. Arsenal.
Shelby, Fort, MI	Detroit.
Shelby, Fort, WI	Prairie du Chien.
Shellbluff, fortifications on, GA	Savannah River, 45 mi. from Augusta.
Shepherd's Fort, WV	Wheeling.
Sheppard, Camp, TX	N of Wichita Falls.
Sherbrooke, Battery, ME	Castine.
Sheridan, Camp, AL	Montgomery.
Sheridan, Camp, NE	W Fork of Beaver Creek, 12 mi. above its mouth.
Sheridan, Camp, VA	Near Winchester.
Sheridan, Camp, WY	Became Ft. Yellowstone.
Sheridan, Fort, IL	Near Highwood.
Sheridan Point, fort at, VA	Ft. Hunt.
Sherman Barracks, NE	A/k/a Omaha Barracks.
Sherman, Battery, MS	Vicksburg.
Sherman, Battery, GA	Tybee Isl.
Sherman, Camp, OH	Chillicothe.
Sherman, Field, MO	NNE Leavenworth.
Sherman, Fort, Panama	Canal Zone.
Sherman, Fort, ID	Coeur d'Alene; ex-Ft. Coeur d'Alene.
Sherman, Fort, SC	Hilton Head.
Sherman, Fort, TN	Chattanooga.
Sherman, Fort, TX	On the Big Cypress in Titus Co.

Sherman Gen. Hospital, TN   Nashville.
Sherrard, Fort, FL
Sherrills Fort, GA   Little River, near Ogeechee.
Sherwood, Battery, CA   At the Presidio.
Shields's Fort, PA   6 mi. from Hannastown.
Shiloh National Cemetery, TN   At Pittsburg Landing.
Ship Island, fort on, MS   12 mi. from Biloxi; a/k/a Ft.
                                      Massachusetts.

Shipp, Battery, NC   At Ft. Caswell.
Shipp, Camp, AL   Anniston.
Shippen, Fort, PA   Near Hannastown.
Shippensburg, fort at, PA
Shipping Point, battery at, VA   Potomac River.
Shirley, Fort, ME   Dresden.
Shirley, Fort, MA   Heath.
Shirley, Fort, PA   Huntingdon Co.; became the later site
                                      of Shirleysburg.

Shullsburg, Fort, WI   Lafayette County.
Shunk, Camp, UT   25 mi. SW of Camp Floyd.
Shurtees Creek, fort at, PA   Ohio River; a little below Pittsburgh.
Sickel Gen. Hospital, VA   Alexandria.
Sidney, Fort, NE   Near Sidney.
Sidney, Fort, VA   Richmond.
Sidney Johnson, Fort, AL   Mobile.
Sigel, Battery, GA   Tybee Isl.
Siguenza, Fort, FL   Santa Rosa Isl.
Siletz, blockhouse at, OR
Sill, Battery, SC   On Rock Creek.
Sill, Camp, TN   Near Murfreesboro.
Sill, Fort, OK   Jct. of Medicine Bluff & Cache Creeks;
                                      ex-Ft. Wichita.
Simcoe, Fort, WA   Klamath Co., in Simcoe Valley, on Yakima
                                      Indian Reservation.

Simmons, Fort, MD   Near Tennallytown, DC.
Simmons, Fort, FL   Caloosahatchie River.
Simon, Camp, PA   Near Harrisburg.
Simon Drum, Fort, FL   Monroe County.
Simon, Fort, GA   See St. Simon.
Simons Gen. Hospital, IL   Mound City.
Simpson, Josiah, Gen. Hospital, VA Near Ft. Monroe.
Simpson's Battery, SC   Charleston.
Sinipee, Fort, WI   Mississippi River, SE part of State.
Sinquefield, Fort, AL   Between Alabama & Tombigbee Rivers.
Sinyakwateen Depot, WA   At Chunikane Bridge.
Sisseton, Fort, ND   Kettle Lake; ex-Ft. Wadsworth.
Sisters of Charity Gen. Hospital, NY Buffalo.
Sisters, The, Reservation, CA   San Francisco Bay.
Sites, Camp, MD   Near Doncaster, Charles Co.
Siverto, Fort, WV   Upper Potomac River.
Six, Number, Battery, KY   At Island #10.
Skagway, Fort, AK   Near Dyea.
Skedaddle, Fort, VA   On Munsons Hill.
Skeel, Camp, MI   3 mi. NW of Oscoda.
Skenesborough, Fort, NY   Lk. Champlain; later the site of Ft.
                                      Whitehall.

Skidaway, Battery, NC   Wilmington River.
Skidaway Narrows, fort at, GA
Skinners Head, battery at, CT
Skocham Bay, fortifications in, WA
Skull Valley, camp in, AZ   Near Prescott.
Sky Harbor AAF, MS   SE of Hattiesburg.
Slaughter, Battery, CA   At the Presidio.
Slemmer, Battery, FL   At Ft. McRee.
Slemmer, Fort, DC   Half mi. E of Soldiers' Home.
Slifer, Camp, PA   Chambersburg.
Sloan Gen. Hospital, VT   Montpelier.
Slocum, Fort, DC   3 mi. N of Washington.
Slocum, Fort, NY   Davids Isl., near New Rochelle.
Slongo, Fort, NY   Nr. present site of Smithtown, a/k/a
                                                  Ft. Salonga.

Slough, Camp, VA   Near Alexandria.
Slough Gen. Hospital, VA   Alexandria.
Slucher, Fort, NY   1 mi. above Niagara Falls.
Smallwood, Fort, MD   Rockpoint, 10 mi. below Baltimore.
Smead, Battery, DC   2 mi. NW of Tennallytown.
Smith, Battery, MD   At Ft. Washington.
Smith, Battery, MS   Near Vicksburg.
Smith, Camp, IL   Near Cairo.
Smith, Camp, WI   Green Bay.
Smith, C.F., Camp, OR   White Horse Creek, nr. the Pueblo mines.
Smith, C.F., Fort, MT   Big Horn River, 8 mi. above mouth of
                                                  Rotten Grass Creek.

Smith, C.F., Fort, VA   Near Aqueduct Bridge, DC.
Smithers, Camp, DE   Near Wilmington.
Smith, Fort, AR   Arkansas River.
Smith, Fort, NC   Near Ft. Fisher.
Smith, Fort, National Cemetery, AR   Arkansas River.
Smith Gen. Hospital, VT   Brattleboro.
Smith, Huntington, Fort, TN   Knoxville.
Smith, J.L., Battery, KY   Near Covington.
Smith, J.R., Fort, FL
Smithland, fortifications at, KY   Mouth of Cumberland River.
Smith's Cantonment, NY   W of Ft. Tompkins.
Smiths Island, battery on, NC   Mouth of Cape Fear River.
Smoky Hill AAF, KS   SSW of Salina.
Snelling, Fort, FL
Snelling, Fort, MN   Near St. Paul; ex-Ft. St. Anthony.
Snyder, Camp, PA   Gettysburg.
Snyder, Fort, DC   Near the insane asylum.
Soldiers' Home National Cemetery, DC   At Soldiers' Home.
Sollers Point, fort at, MD   Ft. Carroll.
Sondrestromfjord Field, Greenland.   Sondrestromfjord.
Sonoma, Camp, CA   Sanoma.
South Aux. Field #5, KS   W of Arkansas City.
South Battery, NY   Governors Isl., NY City harbor.
South Cliff, battery at, NY   Staten Island.
South Dakota State Soldiers' Home, SD   Hot Springs.
Souther AAF, GA   NE of Americus.
Southeast Battery, NY   Governors Isl., NY City harbor.
South Edisto Inlet, fort at, SC
Southern Branch National Soldiers' Home, VA   Elizabeth City County.

South Mortar, Battery, NY	Staten Island.
South Plains AAF, TX	N of Lubbock.
South Point, Battery, MA	Boston harbor.
South Quay Battery, VA	Near Suffolk.
Southworth, Fort, KY	Near Louisville.
Spanish Fort, AL	Near Mobile.
Spanish Fort, LA	Same as Ft. St. John.
Sparks' Fort, PA	Near Burns' Ford, Fayette Co.
Spence Field, GA	SE of Moultrie.
Spencer, Battery, CA	At the Presidio.
Spencer, Redoubt, NY	NY City.
Spesutia Island, fort on, MD	Mouth of Susquehanna River.
Spinola, Fort, NC	Near New Bern.
Spofford Battery, VA	James River.
Spokane AAF, WA	WSW of Spokane.
Spokane Army Depot, WA	Spokane.
Spokane, Fort, WA	Spokane River.
Spotted Tail Agency, SD	White River, 3 mi. W of mouth of Beaver Creek.
Spottsylvania, fort at, VA	
Sprague, Camp, DC	Washington.
Sprague, Camp, NY	Staten Island.
Springs AAF, Camp, MD	Camp Springs.
Spring, Fort, KY	Fayette County.
Spring, Fort, WV	Greenbrier County.
Springdale, Camp, VA	At Ft. Albany.
Springfield Armory, MA	Springfield.
Springfield, camp at, NJ	
Springfield, forts near, MO	Forts #1 to #5.
Springfield National Cemetery, MO	Springfield.
Spring Hill Redoubt, GA	Savannah.
Spring Point, fort at, ME	Ft. Preble.
Springville, fort near, KY	
Spunky, Fort, TX	Hood County.
Squirrel Hill, works on, PA	Pittsburgh.
Stagg Head, fort at, MA	Ft. Conant.
Stambaugh, Camp, WY	In Smiths Gulch, nr. Atlantic City.
Stampers Hill, fort at, RI	Near Providence.
Standing Rock Agency, ND	Became Ft. Yates.
Standing Stone, Fort, PA	Juniata River, Huntingdon Co.
Standish, Fort, MA (#2)	Lovells Isl., 8 mi. from Boston.
Standish, Fort, MA (#1)	Near Plymouth.
Stanford, Fort, AZ	Ex-Ft. Arivaypa; later it became Ft. Breckenridge.
Stanislaus, Camp, CA	Stanislaus River, Stanislaus Co.
Stanley, Camp, TN	Murfreesboro.
Stanley, Camp, TX	Guadelupe River.
Stanley, Fort, FL	
Stanley, Fort, TN	Knoxville.
Stanley Gen. Hospital, NC	New Bern.
Stansbury, Fort, FL	Wakulla River; 9 mi. above St. Marks.
Stanton, Battery, AL	At Ft. Gaines.
Stanton, Battery, GA	Tybee Isl.
Stanton, Battery, MD	Baltimore.

Stanton, Camp, TN	Murfreesboro.
Stanton, Camp, PA	Nr. Girard College, Philadelphia.
Stanton, Camp, VA	Mason's Isl., nr. Georgetown.
Stanton, Fort, DC	Near Uniontown.
Stanton, Fort, NM	Lincoln Co., on the Rio Bonita.
Stanton Gen. Hospital, DC	Washington.
Stanwix, Fort, NY	Rome.
Star, Fort, GA	At Augusta.
Star, Fort, MD	Same as Ft. McHenry.
Starke, Fort, FL	Mouth of Manatee River.
Starkville Aux. AAF, MS	SW of Starkville.
State Corner, Fort, TN	Cumberland Gap.
State Island Reservation, PA	
Statesboro AAF, GA	NE of Statesboro.
Stattler's Fort, PA	Dunkard Creek, Greene Co.
Staunton National Cemetery, VA	Staunton.
Steadman, Battery, TN	Knoxville.
Steadman, Fort, VA	Petersburg.
Stearman, Fort, TN	Near Knoxville.
Steel, Fort, PA	3 mi. E of Mercersburg.
Steele, Battery, NY	At Ft. Terry.
Steele, Camp, CA	Merced River.
Steele, Camp, OR	Mouth of Rattlesnake River.
Steele, Camp, WA	On San Juan Channel.
Steele, Fred, Fort, WY	On N. Platte River.
Steilacoom, Fort, WA	E shore of Puget Sound, Pierce Co.
Stenix, Fort, NY	A/k/a Ft. Stanwix.
Stephen D. Little, Camp, AZ	Nogales.
Stephens, Camp, MO	Became site of Jefferson Barracks.
Stephens, Fort, AL	Alabama River, above Mobile.
Stephens, Fort, LA	At South Pass, Manchac.
Stephens, Fort, MS	Lauderdale Co.
Stephens, Fort, NC	New Bern.
Stephens, Fort, VA	Drurys Bluff.
Stephenson, Fort, NC	New Bern.
Stephenson, Fort, OH	Sandusky Lk.; later the site of Lower Sandusky.
Sternberg Gen. Hospital, GA	Chickamauga.
Steuben, Fort, OH	Later the site of Jeffersonville.
Steuben, Fort, OH	Later the site of Steubenville.
Stevens, Battery, SC	Morris Isl., Charleston harbor.
Stevens, Battery, VA	Suffolk.
Stevens, Camp, FL	Pensacola.
Stevens, Camp, LA	Thibodeaux.
Stevens, Fort, DC	Nr. Soldiers' Home; ex-Ft. Massachusetts.
Stevens, Fort, NM	
Stevens, Fort, NY	Hallets Point, NY City harbor.
Stevens, Fort, OR	Point Adams, mouth of Columbia River, S side.
Stevens, Fort, SC	Near Beaufort.

Stevenson, Battery, MA	At Ft. Warren.
Stevenson, Camp, ID	Boise City.
Stevenson, Fort, AL	Stevenson.
Stevenson, Fort, ND	Missouri River, 70 mi. above Bismarck.
Stevenson Redoubt, TN	Near Chattanooga.
Stewart AAF, Camp, GA	NE of Hinesville.
Stewart Field, NY	W of Newburgh.
Stewart, Fort, GA	Near Savannah.
Stewart, Fort, MT	Missouri River, at mouth of Big Muddy Creek.
Stikine, Fort, AK	Stikine River.
Stinson Aux. Field, MS	NW of Aberdeen.
Stinson Field, TX	S of San Antonio,
Stirling, Fort, NY	Brooklyn Heights, Kings Co.
Stockbridge, fort at, MA	
Stockton Field, CA	S of Stockton.
Stockton, Fort, TX	Comanche Springs, Pecos Co.
Stodderd, Fort, AL	Alabama River, nr. jct. of the Tombigbee.
Stone Gen. Hospital, DC	Washington.
Stoneman, Battery, NY	At Ft. Trrry.
Stoneman, Camp, DC	Giesboro Point.
Stoneman, Camp, DC	Meridian Hill.
Stone River National Cemetery, TN	Murfreesboro.
Stonewall, Fort, AL	Choctaw Bluff.
Stonington, fortifications/arsenal at, CT	
Stono Inlet, fortifications at, SC	
Stono River, fort on, SC	
Stony Point, Fort, NY	Hudson River.
Stony Point, fort on, NY	In the St. Lawrence.
Storey, Fort, VA	Virginia Beach.
Stotsenburg, Battery, CA	At the Presidio.
Stotsenburg, Camp/Fort, Philippines	Pampangs, Luzon.
Stout Field, IN	SW of Indianapolis.
Stout's Fort, MO	St. Charles County.
Strader Gen. Hospital, KY	Louisville.
Strasburg, fort at, VA	
Strawberry Plains, battery at, VA	
Stricker, Battery, MD	At Ft. Howard.
Strong, Camp, NY	Troy.
Strong, Fort, MA (#1)	Noodle Isl., East Boston.
Strong, Fort, MA (#2)	Long Isl. Head, 6 mi. from Boston.
Strong, Fort, NC	Near Wilmington.
Strong, Fort, SC	Morris Isl.
Strong, Fort, VA	1 mi. W of Aqueduct Bridge, DC; ex-Ft. DeKalb.
Strother Field, KS	W of Hackney.
Strother, Fort, AL	Coosa River, near the Ten Islands.
Struthers, Camp, PA	Philadelphia.
Stuart, Battery, NY	At Ft. Totten.
Studdiford, Battery, KY	At Camp Nelson.
Sturgeon Bay, reservation at, WI	
Sturgis AAF, KY	S of Sturgis.

Stuttgart AAF, AR	NW of Stuttgart.
Styles, Battery, SC	James Isl.
Suffolk, Camp, VA	Suffolk.
Suffolk County AAF, NY	Westhampton Beach.
Sugar Hill, Battery, NY	Between Lks. George & Champlain; a/k/a Sugar Loaf Hill.
Sugar House, Fort, SC	Charleston.
Sugar Loaf Battery, NC	Near Wilmington.
Suiter Field, HI	
Sullivan, Battery, ME	At Ft. Williams.
Sullivan, Camp, DC	Washington.
Sullivan, Camp, IN	Near Indianapolis.
Sullivan, Fort, FL	Nr. Hillsboro River, E Florida.
Sullivan, Fort, ME	Moore Isl., Passamaquoddy Bay.
Sullivan, Fort, NH	Trepethen Isl.
Sullivan, Fort, NY	Elmira.
Sullivan, Fort, NC	Roanoke Isl.
Sullivan, Fort, PA	Athens, Bradford Co.
Sullivan, Fort, SC	Charleston harbor.
Sullivans Island, Fort, SC	Charleston harbor; Ft. Moultrie.
Sully, Fort, SD (#1)	Missouri River, 5 mi. above mouth of Cheyenne River.
Sully, Fort, SD (#2)	Cheyenne River, 20 mi. below mouth.
Sulphur Creek, coal reservation, WY	
Summit Gen Hospital, PA	Philadelphia.
Sumner AAF, Fort, NM	At Ft. Sumner.
Sumner Battery, NY	At Ft. Totten.
Sumner, Fort, ME	Portland.
Sumner, Fort, MD	Near Potomac River, above Tennallytown.
Sumner, Fort, NH	Portsmouth.
Sumner, Fort, NM	Guadelupe Co., at the Bosque Redondo on Pecos River.
Sumter, Fort, SC	Charleston harbor.
Sumter fortifications, WI	Sauk County.
Sunbury, fort at, GA	
Sun River, fort at, GA	Ft. Shaw.
Supply, Camp, AZ	Became Camp J. A. Rucker.
Supply, Fort, OK	Between Beaver & Wolf Creeks.
Supply, Fort, UT	At Blacks Fork, near Ft. Bridger.
Susquehanna, Fort, MD	Palmer Isl., Susquehanna River.
Sutters Fort, CA	Nr. Sacramento; a/k/a Ft. Sacramento.
Sttton, Camp, WV	Braxton County.
Suwanee River, fort on, FL	Ft. Macomb.
Swain, Camp, TN	Humboldt.
Swamp Angel Battery, SC	Charleston harbor.
Swan, Fort, PA	Greene County.
Swartz, Fort, PA	Near Milton.
Swearingens Fort, PA	Nr. Morris Crossroads, Fayette Co.
Swatara River, blockhouse on, PA	Lebanon County.
Sweet, Camp, NC	Raleigh.
Sweet, Camp, NC	Salisbury.
Swift, Battery, BC	At Ft. Caswell.
Swift, Camp, NY	West Point.
Swift, Fort, NY	Brooklyn.
Swift Gen. Hospital, WI	Prairie du Chien.

Swords House, camp at, NY   Near Saratoga.
Syberts Fort, VA   Potomac River.
Sykes, Camp, ND   Headwaters of James River.
Syracuse AAF, NY   Syracuse.

An enlisted man's photo sent home to his family just before he went off to fight for the Union in the Civil War.

Table Point Reservation, WA	On Hoods Canal.
Table Rock, Fort, OR	Rogue River, at mouth of Stewarts Creek, Jackson Co.
Taft, Battery, TN	Near Chattanooga.
Talbot, Battery, RI	At Ft. Adams.
Talla Point Reservation, WA	Entrance to Hoods Canal.
Tamhert, Fort, CT	
Tampa Bay, fort at, FL	Ft. Brooke.
Tamrath, Battery, MS	Corinth.
Tanner, Camp, IL	Springfield.
Tanners Creek, battery at, VA	Opp. Craney Isl.
Tar, Fort, VA	Craney Isl., near Norfolk.
Tarentum, blockhouse at, PA	Allegheny River.
Tarpaulin Cove, fortifications at, MA	
Tar River, fort on, NC	In Edgecombe Co.
Tatnall, Fort, GA	Okfenokee Swamp.
Tavern, Fort, FL	In E Florida.
Taylor Barracks/Camp, KY	Louisville.
Taylor, Bob, Camp, TN	Knoxville.
Taylor, Camp, AL	Huntsville.
Taylor, Camp, CA	Pitt River, 8 mi. SE of Ft. Crook.
Taylor, Fort, FL (most recent)	Key West.
Taylor, Fort, FL	Lake Winder.
Taylor, Fort, FL	Hernando County.
Taylor, Fort, LA	Red River, about 60 mi. below Alexandria.
Taylor, Fort, MA	Charlemont, Franklin County.
Taylor, Fort, TX	Rio Grande River; later became site of Ft. Brown.
Taylor, Fort, WA	Snake River, Walla Walla Co.
Taylors Fort, PA	Near Taylorstown.
Taylorsville, fort at, PA	Washington County.
Teconnett, Fort, ME	Kennebec River; became Ft. Halifax.
Teeters Fort, PA	Cross Creek, Washington Co.
Tejon, Fort, CA	Kern Co., near Tejon Pass, 90 mi. N of Los Angeles.
Tellers Point, fort at, NY	Mouth of Croton River.
Tellico Blockhouse, TN	N bank of Tenn. River; opp. old Ft. Loudon.
Temple AAF, TX	NW of Temple.
Ten, Number, Battery, KY	Near Island #10.
Ten, Number, Fort, FL	10 mi. from Palatka.
Tennally, Camp, DC	Tennallytown.
Ten Eyk's Wharf, battery at, NY	NY City.
Terrett, Battery, AL	At Ft. Gaines.
Terrett, Fort, TX	E border of Bexar Co.
Terrill, Battery, DC	1.5 mi. NE of Tennallytown.
Terrill, Camp, VA	Richmond.
Terry, Fort, NY	Plum Island, NE of Long Island.
Ter-waw, Fort, CA	Near Crescent City.
Thayer, Fort, DC	1.5 mi. SW of Bladensburg, MD.
Theodore Winthrop Battery, MA	At Ft. Banks, Grovers Cliff.
Thermal AAF, CA	SW of Thermal.

Thigpens Station, FL	Near New River.
Thomas Barracks, AL	Huntsville.
Thomas, Battery, AL	At Ft. Morgan.
Thomas, Camp, AZ	Apache Co.; became Ft. Apache.
Thomas, Camp, GA	At Chickamauga Park.
Thomas, Camp, OH	4 mi. N of Columbus.
Thomas, Camp, TN	Chattanooga.
Thomas, Fort, KY	3 mi. from Newport.
Thomas, Fort, AZ	Graham County.
Thomas, Fort, VA	Rappahannock River, 5 mi. from Fredericksburg.
Thomas, Geo. H., Fort, ND	Became Ft. Pembina.
Thomas Point, fortifications at, MD	Patuxent River.
Thomasville AAF, GA	NE of Thomasville.
Thompson, Battery, ME	At Ft. McKinley, Grea t Diamond Isl., Portland harbor.
Thompson, Camp, KS	Near Ft. Leavenworth.
Thompson, Fort, ND	Missouri River at Crow Creek Agency.
Thompson, Fort, FL	Caloosahatchie River, near mouth of Lake Flirt.
Thompson, Fort, MO	Near New Madrid.
Thompson, Fort, NC	Near New Bern.
Thompson, Fort, WY	Popo Agie River, Sweetwater Co.
Thompson's Battery, NY	At Horns Hook.
Thorn, Fort, NM	On Rio Grande, at Santa Barbara,
Thornbrough Field, AK	
Thornburgh, Fort, UT	Jct. of DuChesne & Greene Rivers.
Thoulouse, Fort, AL	Later the site of Ft. Jackson, Tuskegee, on Mobile River.
Three Brothers Reservation, CA	Entr. to San Pablo Bay.
Three Forks Owyhee, Camp, ID	Owyhee River; ex-Camp Winthrop.
Three, Number, Battery, KY	Island #10.
Three, Number, Fort, FL	Near Ft. King.
Three, Number, Fort, GA	Near Savannah.
Three, Number, Fort, MA	Charlestown.
Three Sisters Reservation, CA	Entr. to San Pablo Bay.
Three Tree Point Reservation, WA	N bank of Columbia River.
Throgs Neck, fort at, NY	Ft. Schuyler.
Thule Air Base, Greenland	Kap York.
Thunderbolt, Fort, GA	5 mi. SE of Savannah.
Thunderer, Battery, GA	Near Savannah.
Thuillier, Fort, MN	See Ft. L'Huillier.
Ticonderoga, Fort, NY	Lake Champlain; ex-Ft. Carrilow.
Tierandequat, fort at, NY	See Irondequoit.
Tifton Field, GA	SE of Tifton.
Tighlman, Battery, AL	Near Mobile.
Tilden, Fort, NY	Far Rockaway, Queens Co.
Tillinghast, Fort, VA	Near Arlington.
Tilton Gen. Hospital, DE	Wilmington.
Timpanogas, Camp, UT	6 mi. from Provo.
Tinicum Isl., fort on, PA	Ft. Gottenburg.
Tinker Field, OK	E of Oklahoma City.
Tioga Point, fort at, PA	Brafdord Co.
Tirirical Field, Brazil	Sao Luiz.
Titus, Fort, KS	2 mi. from Lecompton.

Tod Barracks, OH	Columbus.
Todd Barracks, DC	Washington.
Todd, Camp, VA	At Ft. Albany.
Tohopeka, Fort, AL	Tallapoosa River.
Toll Gate, Camp, AZ	40 mi. NW of Prescott; became Camp Hualpai.
Tomany Hill, Fort, RI	Newport harbor.
Tomb Hill, Fort, RI	Newport harbor.
Tombigbee, Fort, AL	Little Tombigbee River.
Tombigbee, Fort, AL	Dauphine Isl., later to become site of Ft. Gaines.
Tomlinson's Fort, WV	Grave Creek, Marshall Co.
Tompkins, Camp, WV	On Gauley Mountain.
Tompkins, Fort, GA	E of Okefinokee Swamp.
Tompkins, Fort, FL	8 mi. W of Colerain.
Tompkins, Fort, NY (most recent)	Staten Island, at Ft. Wadsworth.
Tompkins, Fort, NY	Plattsburgh.
Tompkins, Fort, NY	Sacket Harbor.
Toms River, blockhouse on, NJ	
Tongass, Fort, AK	Tongass Islands.
Tongue River Agency, camp at, MT	Camp Merritt.
Tongue River Cantonment, MT	Became Ft. Keogh.
Tonopah AAF, NV	WSW of Tonopah.
Tonopah Aux. Field #5, NV	SW of Tonopah.
Tonyn, Fort, FL	St. Matys River.
Topeka AAF, KS	S of Topeka.
Topsail Inlet, fort at, SC	Ft. Beaufort.
Topsham, Fort, ME	Near Brunswick.
Torbert, Battery, DE	Ft. Delaware.
Tortugas, Dry, fort at, FL	Ft. Jefferson.
Tortuguero, Camp, Puerto Rico	
Totonnock, Fort, ME	Kennebec River.
Totten, Battery, GA	Tybee Island.
Totten, Camp, MO	Franklin.
Totten, Fort, DC	2.5 mi. N of Washington.
Totten, Fort, NY	Willets Point, Flushing, Queens Co.
Totten, Fort, ND	Benson Co., SE shore of Devils Lake.
Totten, Fort, NC	Near New Bern.
Totten Gen. Hospital, KY	Louisville.
Toulouse, Fort, AL	E bank of Coosa River; 34 mi. above jct. with Tallapoosa.
Tousard, Battery, RI	At Ft. Getty.
Tower Island Reservation, AL	In Mobile Bay.
Townsend, Camp, NY	Peekskill.
Townsend, Fort, WA	Near Port Townsend.
Towson, Battery, MD	At Ft. Carroll.
Towson, Fort, I.T. (OK)	In Choctaw Nation.
Towson's Battery, PA	Near Ft. Erie.
Tracey (Tracy), Fort, AL	Near mouth of Tensas.
Traders Hill, post at, GA	St. Marys River.
Travis, Fort, TX	Bolivar Point, Galveston Bay.
Trenholm, Fort, SC	Charleston harbor.
Trentom Barracks, NJ	Trenton.
Trepethen Island, fort on, NH	Ft. Sullivan.
Trial, Fort, VA	Smiths River.

Trinidad, Camp, TX	Lake Trinidad.
Trinity Church, battery at, NY	NY City.
Trinity, Fort, DE	New Castle.
Tripler Army Medical Center, HI	At Ft. Shafter.
Tripler Gen. Hospital, OH	Columbus.
Truax Field, WI	N of Madison.
Trucker's Fort, PA	Near Lehigh Gap.
Trumbull, Fort, CT	New London.
Truson, Fort, AL	Near Spanish Fort.
Tryon, Fort, NY	Washington Heights, NY City.
Tulare, Camp, CA	Tulare County.
Tularosa, Fort, NM	Otero County.
Tunnell, Camp, DE	Middletown.
Turan, Fort, TX	Angelina County.
Turchin, Camp, TN	Murfreesboro.
Turkey Hill, redoubts at, RI	
Turnbull, Camp, VA	Arlington.
Turner Field, GA	ENE of Albany.
Turner's Lane Gen. Hospital, PA	Philadelphia.
Turner's Rock Battery, GA	Near Savannah.
Turtle Creek, works on, PA	Near Pittsburgh.
Turtle Island, battery on, GA	Savannah River.
Tuscarora Valley, blockhouse in, PA	Opp. Mexico, Juniata Co.
Tuskegee AAF, AL	W of Chehaw.
Twiggs, Camp, MS	East Pascagoula.
Twiggs. Fort, MS	Ship Isl.
Two, Number, Battery, KY	Island #10.
Two, Number, Fort, FL	Became Ft. Vinton.
Two, Number, Fort, GA	Savannah.
Two, Number, Fort, MA	Charles River.
Tybee Barracks, GA	Savannah.
Tybee Island, fort on, GA	Ft. Screven.
Tyler, Camp, IL	Chicago.
Tyler, Camp, VA	Fairfax.
Tyler, Fort, AL	Chambers County.
Tyler, Fort, FL	Hernando County.
Tyler, Fort, GA	West Point.
Tyler, Fort, NY	Gardiners Isl., Eastern Suffolk Co.
Tyler's Battery, SC	James Island.
Tyndale, Camp, MD	Near Point of Rocks.
Tyndall Field, FL	SE of San Blas.

During WWII, members of the 80th Division arrive at Camp Forrest, Tennessee.

Uintah, Fort, UT	Uintah River.
Ulrich, Fort, PA	Near Annville.
Umpqua, Fort, OR	Umpqua City.
Unalaklik, Fort, AK	Mouth of Unalaklik River.
Uncompahgre Cantonment, CO	Became Ft. Crawford.
Underwood, Joe, Camp, KY	25 mi. from Cave City.
Union Battery, SC	Folly Isl.
Union, Camp, CA	Near Sacramento.
Union, Camp, CO	Denver.
Union, Camp, MD	Bladensburg.
Union, Camp, OR	Wasco County.
Union, Camp, PA	Near Schuylkill Falls.
Union, Fort, Arsenal, NM	At Ft. Union.
Union, Fort, NM	Near base of Gallinas (Turkey) Mtns.
Union, Fort, ND	Mouth of Yellowstone.
Union, Fort, VA	Near Suffolk.
Union, Fort, WV	Lewisburg.
Union, Fort, WI	Near Dodgeville.
Union Point, battery at, NC	Near New Bern.
United States Battery, ME	Castine.
United States Powder Depot, NJ	Dover; became Picatinny Arsenal.
United States Veterans Hospital #96, NY	N end of Tupper Lake.
University Gen. Hospital, LA	New Orleans.
Uplandt, Fort, DE	
Upper, Fort, NY	Fulton.
Upper Ashuelot, fort at, NH	
Upper Sandusky, fort at, OH	
Upton, Camp, NY	Yaphank, Suffolk County.
Upton, Emory, Battery	See Emory Upton.
Urinston, Fort, VA	Petersburg.
Utah, Fort, UT	Near Salt Lake City.

Vajean, Camp. IN	Indianapolis.
Val de Caens Field, Brazil	Belem.
Valdosta Aux. Field, GA	S of Valdosta.
Valley Forge, camp at, PA	Chester County.
Valley, Fort, GA	Houston County.
Vallonia, Fort, IN	Near Brownstown.
Van Buren Gen. Hospital, LA	At Millikens Bend.
Vance Field, OK	Enid.
Vance's Fort, PA	Cross Creek, Washington Co.
Van Courtland, Fort, FL	Nr. St. Johns River, at head of Kingsbys Pond.
Vancouver Arsenal, WA	Vancouver.
Vancouver Barracks/Fort, WA	Vancouver; ex-Columbia Barracks.
Vanderhorst Wharf, battery at, SC	Charleston harbor.
Van Metre's Fort, WV	Short Creek, Brooke Co.
Van Rensselaer, Fort, NY	Canajoharie.
Van Rensselaer, Fort, NY	Ogdensburg.
Van Schaicks Island, camp on, NY	Jct. of Mohawk & Hudson.
Van Swearingen, Battery, FL	At Ft. Pickens.
Van Swearingen, Fort, FL	Near Lake Okeechobee.
Varnum, Battery, RI	At Ft. Wetherill.
Vass's Fort, VA	
Vaux's Fort, NC	Roanoke River.
Veile, Camp, VA	3 mi. from Norfolk.
Velasco, Fort, TX	Mouth of Brazos River.
Venango, Fort, PA	Venango.
Vengeance, Fort, VT	See Ft. Mott.
Venice AAF, FL	S of Venice.
Venus Point, battery at, GA	Jones Isl., Savannah River.
Verde, Camp, TX	60 mi. NW of San Antonio.
Verde, Fort, AZ	Verde Creek, 30 mi. from Prescott; ex-Camp Lincoln.
Vergennes, arsenal at, VT	Champlain Arsenal.
Vermont, Battery, DC	Near Washington.
Vermont State Soldiers' Home, VT	Bennington.
Vernam Field, British West Indies	Jamaica.
Vernon, Camp, VA	Near Ft. Ellsworth.
Verplanck Point, forts at, NY	Fts. Lafayette & Fayette.
Vest, Camp, MO	4 mi. from Boonville.
Vichy AAF, MO	N of Vichy.
Vicksburg National Cemetery, MS	Vicksburg.
Victorville Army Flying School, CA	6 mi. W of Victorville.
Vidalia Aux. AAF, GA	SE of Vidalia.
Vide-Poche, Camp, MS	Near Rocky Springs.
Vieux Desert Island, fort on, WI	Wisconsin River.
Vieux Fort, British West Indies	St. Lucia.
Vigilance, Camp, NM	Near Albuquerque.
Vigo, Camp, IN	Terre Haute.
Vincent AAF, AZ	SSE of Yuma.
Vint Hill Farms, VA	Warrenton.
Vinton, Fort, FL	18 mi. NW of Indian River Inlet.
Virginia, Camp, VA	White Sulphur Springs.
Virginia, Fort, NY	Sacket Harbor.

Virginia Key Reservation, FL	Biscayne Bay, S of Miami.
Virginia Point, battery at, TX	5 mi. from Galveston.
Visalia AAF, CA	W of Visalia.
Volunteer, Fort, NY	Sacket Harbor.
Von Schrader Barracks, KY	Louisville.
Voorhees, Camp, NJ	Sea Girt.
Vose, Fort, FL	Nr. Aucilla River; 22 mi. from Tallahassee.
Voskressenski, Fort, AK	Near Kenayaw Bay.
Vulcan, Fort, GA	Jones Isl., Savannah River.

Major General Robert F. Frederick, a recipient of the Air Medal during WWII. He was a member of the First Special Service Force.

Waadah Island Reservation, WA	E side of Neah Harbor.
Wabash, Fort, IN	Mouth of Wabash River.
Wacaco Blockhouse, PA	Near Philadelphia.
Wacahoota, Fort, FL	9 mi. SW of Micanopy.
Wacissa, Fort, FL	Mouth of Wacissa River.
Waco AAF, TX	NE of Waco.
Waddy, Fort, SC	Near Charleston.
Wade, Camp. I.T. (OK)	Near Lisbon.
Wade, Fort, FL	
Wadsworth, Camp, KY	At Hazel Green.
Wadsworth, Camp, VA	Near Langley.
Wadsworth, Camp, VA	On Uptons Hill.
Wadsworth, Camp, SC	Spartanburg.
Wadsworth, Fort, NY	Staten Island, at The Narrows; ex-Ft. Richmond.
Wadsworth, Fort, ND	Became Ft. Sisseton.
Wadsworth, Fort, VA	Near Petersburg.
Wagner, Fort, DC	Good Hope Hill; ex-Ft. Good Hope.
Wagner, Fort, SC	Morris Island.
Walbach, Battery, RI	At Ft. Wetherill.
Walbach, Camp, FL	At Ft. Myers.
Walbach, Camp, WY	Lodge Pole Creek, nr. Cheyenne Pass.
Walcott, Battery, MA	At Ft. Rodman.
Walcott, Fort, RI	Goat Isl., Narragansett Bay.
Walesboro Field, IN	W of Walesboro.
Walker, Battery, VA	
Walker, Camp, MD	Salisbury.
Walker, Fort, FL	W of Orange Lake.
Walker, Fort, GA	Near Okefinokee Swamp.
Walker, Fort, SC	Hilton Head; became Ft. Wells.
Walker's Fort, TX	Brazos River.
Wallace, Battery, CA	At Ft. McDowell.
Wallace, Camp, ID	Alturas County.
Wallace, Camp, MO	Lexington.
Wallace, Camp, OH	Near Columbus.
Wallace, Fort, KS	S Fork of Smoky Hill River.
Wallace, Fort, PA	Near Blairsville.
Walla Walla AAF, WA	NE of Walla Walla.
Walla Walla, Fort, WA	Walla Walla.
Wallen, Camp, AZ	Badocomari Creek, 65 mi. SE of Tucson.
Wallenpaupack, Fort, PA	Pike County.
Waller Field, Trinidad	Cumuto.
Walnut Hills, fort at, MS	Ft. Adams.
Walnut Ridge AAF, AR	NE of Walnut Ridge.
Walpack, Fort, PA	Delaware River.
Walpole, fort at, NH	
Walterboro AAF, SC	NE of Walterboro.
Walter Reed Gen. Hospital, DC	Washington.
Walthour's Fort, PA	8 mi. W of Greensburg.
Walton, Fort, FL	On Santa Rosa Sound.
Wampler, Battery, SC	James Island.
Wappoo, Battery, SC	James Island.

Warburton, Fort, MD	Became Ft. Washington.
Ward, Battery, MA	At Ft. Strong.
Ward, Camp, MI	Detroit.
Ward, Fort, FL	Mouth of Olustee Creek.
Ward, Fort, VA	3 mi. NW of Alexandria,
Ward Gen. Hospital, MJ	Newark.
Wardner, Camp, ID	Kellogg.
Wardon's Fort, WV	Lost River.
Wards Hill, battery at, VA	Near Richmond.
Wardwell, Camp, CO	Became Ft. Morgan.
Waring, Battery, NC	Charleston.
Warner, Camp, OR	20 mi. from Warner Lake.
Warren, Fort, MA (#1)	Governors Isl., after Ft. Winthrop.
Warren, Fort, MA (#2)	Georgies Isl., Boston harbor.
Warren, Fort, NC	Plymouth.
Warren, Fort, VT	Castleton.
Warren, Francis E. Warren, Fort, WY	Cheyenne.
Warrenton, Camp, VA	Near Sulphur Springs.
Warsaw Sound. works at, GA.	
Warwick, battery at, VA	
Warwick Neck, battery at, RI	
Washakie, Fort, WY	Shoshone Indian Reservation; ex-Ft. Augur.
Washburn, Camp, WI	Milwaukee.
Washington Arsenal, DC	Became Washington Barracks.
Washington Barracks, DC	Washington.
Washington, Camp, NJ	Trenton.
Washington, Camp, NC	Portsmouth.
Washington, Camp, PA	Near Easton.
Washington, fort at, GA	
Washington, Fort, MD	Potomac River, mouth of Piscataway Creek; site of old Ft. Warburton.
Washington, Fort, NH	Portsmouth.
Washington, Fort, NY	NY City.
Washington, Fort, NC	Washington.
Washington, Fort, OH	Cincinnati.
Washington, Fort, OR	Nootka Sound.
Washington, Fort, PA	Montgomery Co., 8 mi. E of Norristown.
Washington, Fort, PA	Opp. Harrisburg.
Washington, Fort, RI	See Ft. George.
Washington, Fort, TX	Pass Cavallo.
Washington Gen. Depot, VA	Alexandria; became Washington Quartermaster Depot.
Washington Gen. Hospital, TN	Memphis.
Washington Park Gen. Hospital, OH	Cincinnati,
Washington Quartermaster Depot, VA	Alexandria; became Cameron Station.
Washington State Soldiers' Home, WA	Orting.
Washita, Fort, I.T. (OK)	Near False Washita River, 25 mi. above its mouth.
Warsaw Island, fortifications on, SC	
Watauga, Fort, TN	Elizabethtown.
Waterbury's Battery, NY	NY City.
Wateree Ford, battery at, SC	
Waterford Arsenal, PA	Waterford.
Watertown AAF, SD	Watertown.

Watertown Arsenal, MA	Watertown.
Watervliet Arsenal, NY	West Troy.
Watson, Camp, OR	John Day River.
Watson, Fort, SC	On Wrights Bluff, near Scotts Lake.
Watson Laboratories, NJ	Eatontown.
Waycross AAF, GA	N of Waycross.
Wayne, Fort, GA	Near Brunswick.
Wayne, Fort, IN	Maumee River, site of present city of this name.
Wayne, Fort, I.T. (OK)	Illinois River, near MO State border.
Wayne, Fort, MI	Detroit.
Webb, Fort, NY	Near West Point.
Webster, Fort, NM	Became Ft. McLane.
Webster Gen. Hospital, NH	Manchester.
Webster Gen. Hospital, TN	Memphis.
Weed, Battery, NY	At Ft. Wadsworth.
Weed, Fort, VA	Near Washington, DC.
Weightman, Camp, MO	Near Springfield.
Wekiwa, Fort, FL	1 mi. above mouth of Spring Creek.
Weller, Fort, CA	Russian River, 50 mi. from Cloverdale.
Wellston Depot, GA	Became Robins Field.
Wells, Fort, SC	Ex-Ft. Walker.
Wells's Fort, PA	Washington County.
Wendover Field, UT	SSE of Wendover.
Wessells, Fort, NC	Plymouth.
West Buildings Gen. Hospital, MD	Baltimore.
Westcott, Fort, FL	In the Everglades.
West End Gen. Hospital, OH	Cincinnati.
Western Branch National Mil. Home, KS	Leavenworth County.
Western, Fort, ME	Augusta.
Westfall's Fort, WV	
Westfield Reservation, NJ	
West, Fort, NM	Headwater of the Gila River.
West Head, battery at, MA	
West Head, battery at, NY	
Westover Field, MA	Springfield.
West Point, Military Academy at, NY	United States Military Academy.
West's Fort, WV	Lewis County.
Wetherill, Camp, KY	Ft. Thomas.
Wetherill, Camp, SC	Greenville.
Wetherill, Fort, RI	Conanicut Isl., Narragansett Bay.
Weymouth Battery, ME	At Ft. McKinley, Portland harbor.
Wheadmans, Fort, FL	
Wheeler, Camp, GA	Macon.
Wheeler, Camp, AL	Huntsville.
Wheeler Field, HI	S of Wahiawa, Oahu.
Wheeler, Fort, PA	Columbia County.
Wheeler-Sack Aux. AAF, NY	At Ft. Drum, Watertown.
Wheeling, fort at, WV	Bonnett's Fort.
Wheelock, Fort, FL	Orange Lake.
Wheelus Field, Lybia	Tripoli.
Whetstone Agency, SD	Missouri River, 30 mi. from Ft. Randall.
Whidbys Island, fort on, WA	Ft. Nugen.
Whipple, Camp, FL	Pease Creek.
Whipple, Fort/Barracks, AZ	Prescott.

Whipple, Fort, VA	Arlington Hts.; became Ft. Myer.
White Battery, MD	At Ft. Washington.
White, Fort, AL	Clarke County.
Whitehall, blockhouse at, NY	
White Point, fort at, SC	Near Charleston.
White Sands Missile Range, NM	Near Las Cruces.
White's Fort. TN	Knoxville.
Whiteside, Camp, KS	Ft. Riley.
Whitman, Fort, WA	
Whittlesey, Fort, KY	Near Newport.
Whitworth, Fort, VA	Petersburg; a/k/a Ft. Alexander.
Wicassett, fort at, ME	See Sheepscot Bay.
Wichita, Camp, I.T. (OK)	Became Ft. Sill.
Wickliffe, Camp, KY	Green River.
Wigfall, Camp, VA	Near Bull Run.
Wikoff (Wyckoff), Camp, NY	Montauk, became Camp Hero.
Wilburn, Fort, IL	Illinois River, nr. Peru.
Wilbur Wright Field, OH	NE of Dayton; became Patterson Fld.
Wilcox, Battery, VA	James River.
Wilcox, Camp, TX	Trinity River.
Wildcat, Camp, KY	Near London.
Wilder, Camp, TN	Knoxville.
Wilhelm, Battery, WA	At Ft. Flagler.
Wilhelms, Fort, NY	In Hudson River.
Wilkes-Barre, forts at, PA	Fts. Dickinson & Lillope.
Wilkeson, Battery, CA	At Ft. Rosecrans.
Wilkin, Battery, MD	At Ft. Washington.
Wilkins, Fort, GA	Oconee River.
Wilkins, Fort, MI	On Lk. Superior at Copper Mine Harbor.
Wilkinson, Camp, MN	Leech Lake.
Wilkinson, Fort, GA	Oconee River, nr. Milledgeville.
Willard, Fort, VA	Near Alexandria.
Willets Point, fort at, NY	Ft. Totten, Queens County.
William and Mary, Fort, MA	Near Boston.
William Augustus, Fort, NY	Near Ogdensburg.
William Castle, Fort, MA	In Boston harbor.
William, Fort, GA	Near Cumberland Isl.
William, Fort, MA	Near Boston.
William, Fort, MN	
William, Fort, NH	Grand Isl., mouth of Piscataqua.
William, Fort, NC	Near Plymouth.
William, Fort, PA	Near Schuylkill River.
William Hendrick, Fort, NY	At Bowling Green, NY City.
William Henry, Fort, ME	Pemaquid.
William Henry, Fort, NY	S end of Lake George.
William McKinley, Fort, Philippines	Rizal.
William Penn, Camp, PA	Chelten Hills.
Will Rogers Field, OK	SW of Oklahoma City.
Williams AAF, Camp, AZ	N of Camp Douglas.
Williamsburg, fort at, VA	Ft. Magruder.
Williams, Camp, UT	Near Salt Lake City.
Williams, Camp, VA	Near Richmond.
Williams, Castle, NY	Governors Isl., NY City harbor.
Williams Field, AZ	E of Higley.
Williams, Fort, AL	Coosa River, mouth of Cedar Creek.

Williams, Fort, CO	Arkansas River.
Williams, Fort, FL	
Williams, Fort, ME	At Portland Head.
Williams, Fort, MS	Near Corinth.
Williams, Fort, NY	Mohawk River.
Williams, Fort, VA	On Traitors Hill, nr. Alexandria.
Willow Grove, Camp, AZ	78 mi. W of Ft. Mojave.
Wilson, Camp, TX	San Antonio.
Wilmer, Camp, MD	Pimlico.
Wilmington Arsenal, DE	Wilmington.
Wilmington National Cemetery, NC	Wilmington.
Wilson, Fort, MI	
Wilson Point Reservation, WA	
Wilson's Fort, WV	
Wiltsee, Battery, TN	Knoxville.
Winchester, Battery, MD	At Ft. Armistead.
Winchester, Fort, OH	Auglaize River.
Winchester National Cemetery, VA	Winchester.
Winder, Camp, VA	Near Richmond.
Windmill Point, battery at, MD	Near Annapolis.
Windsor Field, Bahamas	Nassau.
Winfield, Camp, NC	Near Hatteras Inlet.
Winfield Scott, Camp, NV	In Paradise Valley.
Winfield Scott, Camp, VA	Near Yorktown.
Winfield Scott, Fort, CA	At the Presidio; ex-Ft. Point.
Wingate, Fort, NM	Headwaters of Rio Puerco; site of old Ft. Lyon.
Winnebago Agency, MN	
Winnebago, Fort, WI	On Fox River.
Winslow, Fort, NY	Hudson River, above Mohawk.
Wint, Fort, Philippines	Grande Isl., Subic Bay.
Winter Hill, fortifications on, MA	Charlestown.
Winter Island, fort on, MA	Ft. Pickering, Salem harbor.
Wintermoot's Fort, PA	In Wyoming Valley, nr. Sturmerville.
Winthrop, Camp, ID	Became Camp Three Forks Owyhee.
Winthrop, Camp, VA	Near Richmond.
Winthrop, Fort, MA	Governors Isl., Boston harbor, site of old Ft. Warren.
Winthrops Point, fort at, NH	
Winthrop, Theodore, Battery, MA	At Ft. Banks, Grovers Cliff.
Winyaw Bay, redoubts at, SC	
Winyaw, Fort, SC	At Blythe's Point, nr. Georgetown.
Wiscasset, Fort, ME	At Sheepscot Bay.
Wisconsin Point Reservation, WI	
Wisconsin State Soldiers' Home, WI	Waupaca.
Wise, Fort, PA	Washington County.
Wisewell Barracksm DC	Washington.
Witchen, Battery, VA	Near Deep Bottom.
Wolcott, Fort, RI	Goat Isl., Newport harbor.
Wolff's Fort, PA	Washington County.
Wolford, Camp, KY	Near Somerset.
Wolf Run Battery, VA	Occoquan River.
Wolters, Camp, TX	16 mi. N of Weatherford.
Wood, A.E., Camp, CA	In Yosemite National Park.

Wood, Battery, VA	James River.
Woodbury, Fort, VA	Near Aqueduct Bridge.
Wood, Camp, VA	Arlington.
Wood, Camp, TX	S of Barksdale.
Wood, Camp, TX	Neuces River.
Wood, Fort, LA	At Chef Menteur; became Ft. Macomb.
Wood, Fort, NY	Bedloes Isl., NY City harbor.
Wood, Fort, TN	Near Chattanooga.
Wood, George, Camp, KY	Mumfordsville.
Wood, G.W.F., Camp, TX	50 mi. NW of Ft. Inge.
Wood, Leonard, Fort, MO	St. Robert; a/k/a Ft. Wood.
Wood National Cemetery, NY	Elmira.
Wood, Redoubt, MD	
Woodruff, Fort, VA	Near Portsmouth.
Woodward AAF, OK	NW of Tangier.
Wool, Camp, MA	Worcester.
Wool, Camp, NC	Hatteras Inlet.
Wool, Fort, CA	Mouth of Trinity River.
Wool, Fort, FL	Suwanee River, 10 mi. above its mouth.
Wool, Fort, VA	On the Rip Raps, nr. Ft. Monroe.
Wooster, Battery, RI	At Ft. Mansfield.
Wooster, Fort, CT	New Haven harbor.
Worden, Fort, AK	
Worden, Fort, WA	At Point Wilson, nr. Port Townsend.
Worth AAF, Fort, TX	W of City.
Worth, Battery, FL	At Ft. Pickens.
Worth, Camp, TN	Cherokee County.
Worth, Fort, TX	Tarrant Co, on Trinity River.
Worth, Fort, VA	Near Alexander.
Worthington, Fort, MD	Near Baltimore.
Wrangell, Fort, AK	Wrangell Island.
Wright, Battery, SC	James Island.
Wright, Camp, AZ	Near Warner's Ranch.
Wright, Camp, CA	Near Warner's Ranch.
Wright, Field, AL	Became Maxwell AAF.
Wright, Fort, CA	In Round Valley.
Wright, Fort, TN	Mississippi River, nr. Ft. Pillow.
Wright, Fort, WA	Near Spokane.
Wright, Gen. Hospital, CA	San Francisco.
Wright, H.G., Fort, NY	Fishers Isl., NE of Long Island.
Wyllys, Fort, NY	Hudson River, nr. West Point.
Wyoming, Fort, PA	Near Wilkes-Barre.
Wyoming State Soldiers' Home, WY	Cheyenne.

Yakutat Bay, fort on, AK — Yakutat Bay.
Yam Hill, Fort, OR — Near McMinnville.
Yarmouth, fort at, ME
Yates, Camp, IL — Near Springfield.
Yates, Fort, ND — At Standing Rock Indian Agency.
Yazoo City, fort at, MS
Yellow Bayou, fortifications at, LA
Yellow Medicine, Camp, MN — At Upper Sioux Agency.
Yellowstone, Fort, WY — In Yellowstone National Park; ex-Camp Sheridan.

Yerba Buena Island Reservation, CA — San Francisco harbor.
York, fortifications at, ME
York, Fort, VA — York River.
Yorktown National Cemetery, VA — Yorktown.
Yosemite National Park, reservation/camp in, CA
Young, Fort, WV
Young, S.B.M., Camp, GA — Augusta.
Yucca AAF, AZ — NE of Yucca.
Yukon, Fort, AK — Yukon River.
Yuma AAF, AZ — SSE of Yuma; became Vincent AAF.
Yuma, Fort, CA — Colorado River, opp. mouth of the Gila.
Yuma Test Branch, AZ — Yuma.

Zabriski's Redoubt, NC — On Cobbs Hill.
Zabrisky, Fort, VA — Near Zabriski River.
Zarah, Fort, KS — Walnut Creek, 2 mi. above its mouth.
Zandry Field, Surinam
Zeeks Island, battery on, NC — Mouth of Cape Fear River.
Zeller, Fort, PA — Near Newmansville.
Zephyrhills AAF, FL — SE of Zephyrhills.
Zimmerman, Fort, NY — St. Johnsville.
Zoellner, Battery, TN — Knoxville.
Zollersville, Fort, PA — Zollersville.
Zollicoffer, Camp, TN — 3 mi. S of Livingston.
Zollicoffer, Fort, TN — 5 mi. below Nashville.
Zumwalls, Fort, MO — St. Charles County.